D1249898

An Employer's Guide To EMPLOYMENT LAW ISSUES IN MINNESOTA

Tenth Edition

February 2009

A Collaborative Effort
Minnesota Department of Employment and Economic Development
Lindquist & Vennum P.L.L.P.

ACKNOWLEDGMENTS

The Minnesota Small Business Assistance Office is pleased to join with the Minneapolis law firm of Lindquist & Vennum P.L.L.P. in this collaborative publication. Particular thanks go to Robert V. Atmore, Ansis V. Viksnins, Wallace G. Hilke and Marnie L. DeWall of the Employment Shareholder Group of Lindquist & Vennum P.L.L.P., Nancy S. Flury, Nancy B. Vollertsen and Edward J. Wegerson of the Employee Benefits, Executive Compensation and Employment Law Group of Lindquist & Vennum P.L.L.P., Kurtis A. Greenley of the Products Liability Group of Lindquist & Vennum P.L.L.P., Bruce H. Little of the Intellectual Property Group of Lindquist & Vennum P.L.L.P., Barbara Wood and Ryan McGary of the Health Law and Practice Group of Lindquist & Vennum P.L.L.P., Joann Kunjummen of Lindquist & Vennum P.L.L.P., and to Madeline Harris and Mark Simmer of the Minnesota Small Business Assistance Office.

Please be sure to look at our Disability Discrimination section and Leaves of Absence and Time Off section, which include updates on the Americans with Disabilities Act (ADA) and the Family and Medical Leave Act (FMLA), respectively.

Charles A. Schaffer
Minnesota Small Business Assistance Office

TABLE OF CONTENTS

INTRODUCTION

This Guide is designed to alert Minnesota employers to issues which commonly arise in the workplace. It should be used only as a guide and not as a definitive source to answer your legal questions. The scope of the remarks contained in this Guide are largely based upon the authors' own experiences dealing with employment law issues and are aimed primarily at private employers whose workplace practices are not subject to collective bargaining agreements. Employers who are subject to collective bargaining agreements will also be subject to most of the rules set forth in this Guide in addition to the applicable collective bargaining agreements.

Whenever an employer needs to make an employment decision, various factors will affect that decision. Every situation is different. Therefore, as emphasized throughout this Guide, consultation with legal counsel is strongly advised as you encounter situations in the workplace which you must address. We hope that this Guide will raise questions and familiarize you with frequently arising employment law issues so that you will know when to seek professional advice before a workplace decision becomes a problem. This is the tenth edition of what is a periodically updated Guide to assist Minnesota employers.

Prior editions are superseded by this edition and are no longer deemed definitive. This edition is designed to reflect the law as it existed through the Fall of 2008, although where possible, the authors have incorporated more recent changes in the law. Employment law is a rapidly changing area of the law, and what is true today may not have been true yesterday and may not be true tomorrow. Again, your own legal counsel should be consulted as you make your employment decisions. Lindquist and Vennum and the Minnesota Small Business Assistance office cannot and do not assume responsibility for employment decisions based upon the information provided in this Guide.

THE HIRING PROCESS

THE EMPLOYMENT RELATIONSHIP

This book is designed to be an employment law resource for Minnesota business owners. Before delving into the law surrounding the employment relationship, however, the business owner must determine whether the individuals it has retained to perform services are employees or independent contractors. Business owners who use independent contractors may think they do not have employees and, therefore, that employment laws do not apply to them. An individual's status as an independent contractor, however, is not determined by agreement or by what he or she is called. Rather, the individual's status is determined by what he or she actually does. If an individual performing services for a business is being treated as an independent contractor, but is performing the work of an employee, and an agency such as the Internal Revenue Service or the Minnesota Department of Revenue discovers this error, the results can be expensive to the business.

Before designating an individual as an employee or an independent contractor, the business owner should consider the following factors:

- **Instructions.** A worker who is required to comply with another person's instructions about when, where, and how he or she is to work is ordinarily an employee.

- **Training.** Training a worker by, e.g., requiring an experienced employee to work with him or her, corresponding with the worker, or requiring the worker to attend meetings, weighs in favor of employee status because the employer for whom the services are performed wants the services performed in a particular method or manner.

- **Integration.** A worker is subject to direction and control if his or her services are integrated into the company's business operations. Thus, this factor weighs in favor of an employment relationship.

- **Services Rendered Personally.** If the worker must perform the agreed upon services personally, this factor weighs in favor of employee status because presumably the employer is interested in the method used to accomplish the work as well as the results.

- **Hiring, Supervising and Paying Assistants.** If the business owner hires, supervises and pays workers' assistants, this factor generally shows control over the workers on the job. If, however, one worker hires, supervises, and pays assistants pursuant to a contract under which the worker agrees to provide materials and labor and under which the worker is responsible only for the attainment of a result, independent contractor status is indicated.

- **Continuing Relationship.** A continuing relationship between the employer and the worker weighs in favor of an employment relationship.

- **Set Hours of Work.** This is a factor indicating control and, therefore, an employment relationship.

- **Full Time Required.** If the worker must devote substantially full time to the business, an employment relationship is indicated because the employer has control over the amount of time the worker spends working and therefore can restrict the worker from doing other gainful work. An independent contractor would be free to work when and for whom he or she chooses.

- **Doing Work on the Employer's Premises.** Work performed on the employer's premises suggests control over the worker, especially if the work could be done elsewhere. Work done off the premises indicates some freedom from control. This fact alone, however, does not mean that the worker is not an employee. The importance of this factor depends on the nature of the service involved and the extent to which an employer generally would require employees to perform such services on the employer's premises.

- **Order or Sequence of Work.** Requiring a worker to perform services in an order or sequence set by the employer shows that the worker is not free to follow the worker's own pattern but must follow established routines and schedules of the employer. Thus, this factor weighs in favor of an employment relationship.

- **Oral or Written Reports.** Requiring oral or written reports indicates a degree of control by the employer and, thus, an employment relationship.

- **Payment by Hour, Week, Month.** Payment by the hour, week, or month generally points to an employer-employee relationship. Payment by fee generally indicates an independent contractor relationship.

- **Payment of Business and/or Traveling Expenses.** If the employer pays the worker's business and/or traveling expenses, this factor weighs heavily in favor of an employer-employee relationship.

- **Benefits.** The provision of benefits such as insurance, a pension plan, PTO vacation pay, and sick pay indicate an employer-employee relationship.

- **Furnishing of Tools and Materials.** If the employer furnishes significant tools, materials, and other equipment, this tends to show the existence of an employment relationship.

- **Significant Investment.** If the worker invests in facilities that are used by the worker in performing services and the facilities are of the kind that are not typically maintained by employees, that factor tends to indicate independent contractor status. Lack of investment in facilities indicates dependence on the employer and, therefore, the existence of an employment relationship.

- **Realization of Profit or Loss.** The worker's ability to realize a profit or suffer a loss is indicative of independent contractor status. In other words, if the worker is subject to real risk of economic loss due to significant investments or bona fide liabilities for expenses, this factor indicates that the worker is an independent contractor. The risk that the worker may not be paid for his or her services is not a sufficient economic risk to support independent contractor status.

- **Working for More Than One Company at a Time.** If a worker performs services for a variety of unrelated persons or companies at the same time, he or she is most likely an independent contractor. It is possible, however, that an individual who performs services for more than one person or company may be an employee of each of those persons or companies.

- **Making Services Available to the General Public.** If a worker's services are available to the general public on a regular and consistent basis, this factor weighs in favor of independent contractor status.

- **Right to Discharge.** If the employer has the right to discharge the worker in question, this factor indicates that the worker is an employee. A person is an independent contractor if he or she cannot be fired if he or she produces results that meet contract specifications.

- **Right to Terminate.** If the worker has the right to end his or her relationship with the employer for whom the services are performed at any time without incurring liability, this factor indicates an employer-employee relationship.

The above factors are common-law rules that the Internal Revenue Service looks at in determining whether an individual is an employee or an independent contractor.[1] None of the factors discussed above, standing alone, will determine independent contractor or employee status. Each situation is considered on a case-by-case basis,[2] and the IRS, the Minnesota Department of Revenue, and the Minnesota Department of Employment and Economic Development each assign different weights to each factor. The most significant factor with all agencies, however, is the business owner's right to control the individual's method or manner of performance. If the business owner has the right to control the method or manner of performance, then the individual is most likely an employee. If the business owner has the right to control the results of the work, but does not have the right to control the manner and means of accomplishing the result, the individual is most likely an independent contractor. In addition, there are statutory employees[3] for FICA tax purposes (e.g., commission drivers, full-time life insurance sales persons, home-workers and traveling sales persons) and statutory non-employees[4] for FICA, unemployment and income tax purposes (e.g., qualified real estate agents and direct sellers). Business owners are urged to consult their legal counsel before classifying an individual as an independent contractor instead of an employee.

Finally, there are special rules regarding the classification of construction workers. In particular, employers should note that a new state law, effective January 1, 2009, requires individuals (not corporations, LLCs, or partnerships) who work as independent contractors in the building construction industry to obtain from the Department of Labor and Industry an Independent Contractor Exemption Certificate (ICEC). As of January 1, 2009, for purposes of the state's workers' compensation, unemployment insurance, wage and hour, and occupational safety and health laws, individuals doing building construction work without an ICEC will be employees of the contractor for whom they are working.[5]

HIRING IN GENERAL

When an employee is hired in Minnesota, unless the employer and the employee enter into an oral or written employment agreement or a collective bargaining agreement specifying otherwise, that employee is employed "at-will," which means the employer can discharge the employee at any time for any lawful reason and the employee can quit at any time for any reason. (Restrictions on an employer's ability to terminate an at will employee are discussed later in this Guide.) During the hiring process, however, if employers are not cautious, inadvertent contracts can be formed with new employees, and unnecessary information may be elicited from applicants which could later form the basis of a discrimination charge if the applicant is not hired. By keeping these two areas (contracts and discrimination) in mind during the hiring process, employers may avoid a great deal of liability after the hiring process is complete.

During the hiring process, employers also should keep in mind the federal Americans with Disabilities Act ("ADA"), which prohibits disability discrimination during hiring. For example, an employer may not reject a job applicant due to the possible risk of future injury to that applicant or due to the risk that the employer may incur higher insurance costs if the applicant is hired. The ADA applies to employers with 15 or more employees and will be discussed in detail in the Disability Discrimination section of this Guide.

ADVERTISING

If the employer needs to advertise for a position, it should choose the wording it uses in an advertisement carefully. Employers should avoid ambiguous or misleading language which may imply an illegal bias toward any particular group of applicants. It is a violation of the Minnesota Human Rights Act to disclose a preference in an employment advertisement regarding sex, age, race, color, creed, religion, national origin, marital status, status with regard to public assistance, disability, or sexual orientation.[6] If the employer is a federal contractor or subcontractor, the employer may have obligations to advertise the position with the local job service and use the words "equal employment opportunity employer" in an employment advertisement.

THE EMPLOYMENT APPLICATION

The employer must review the employment application carefully. In order to determine whether all the questions asked are appropriate, consider whether the information requested is reasonably related to the job for which the applicant is applying. For example, does the employer really need to know whether an applicant for a custodian position has a driver's license and the number and the state in which it was issued? Also, determine whether any of the questions on the application ask information which might impermissibly reveal the applicant's status as a member of a protected class. For example, inquiries into club memberships or civic organizations should be followed by a disclaimer which states that the applicant need not disclose any activities which might reveal him or her as a member of a protected class.

Employers should not automatically assume that standard, preprinted employment applications only ask legally permissible questions. First, a preprinted form may ask questions which are not reasonably related to the job for which the applicant is applying. Second, preprinted employment applications may not be tailored to comply with individual state laws and may ask impermissible questions as discussed in the Interviewing section later in this Guide.

Employers who are federal, state or local government contractors or who must compile equal employment opportunity (EEO) data on applicants (as may be defined by statute or regulation),[7] may ask certain questions relating to race/ethnicity and gender so long as those questions are asked on a form which is kept completely separate from the employment application and which is not used in the hiring process. Completion of this form by applicants is voluntary.

THE APPLICATION PROCESS

Under the federal Americans with Disabilities Act (discussed in the Disability Discrimination section of this Guide), employers must provide an equal opportunity for individuals with disabilities to participate in the job application process. Therefore, employers subject to the ADA must make reasonable accommodations to enable disabled applicants to apply for available jobs. Employers are not required to make reasonable accommodations in advance; they are simply required to make such accommodations on request.[8] This might include providing job information in an accessible location or providing written job information in various formats (e.g., in large print or on CD).

DISCLAIMERS

Employers should consider including disclaimers on employment applications, in any employee handbook maintained by the employer, and, if there is a handbook, in a separate acknowledgment regarding the handbook. The disclaimer must be clear and conspicuous and should include the following:

- That the employer retains the right to terminate its employees at any time for any reason not prohibited by law, that an employee has the right to resign employment at any time for any reason (subject to the employer's notice request or requirement, if any), and that these mutual rights constitute the employer's at-will employment policy;

- That any understandings and agreements between the employer and any employee to the contrary must be in writing and signed by the proper officer of the company;

- That the employee handbook, if there is one, does not constitute an employment contract for a term of employment and may be revised or discarded at the employer's discretion; and

- That the employee handbook, if it is being newly issued, supersedes all prior handbooks and previously issued policies.

INTERVIEWING

When interviewing a prospective job applicant, the employer should only ask questions which reasonably relate to the job in question. The employer should not request information that is not job-related and must not ask questions that might reveal an applicant's protected status. If discriminatory questions are asked or discussed during an interview, the employer may have to later show that the information obtained was not used to discriminate. With that in mind, it is prudent to avoid certain inquiries completely. For example, employers should not inquire into the following areas:

- Age or date of birth;[9]

- Marital status (this includes whether an applicant is married, divorced, separated, widowed or in the process of having a marriage annulled or dissolved, or the identity of one's current or former spouse, including whether the spouse is an employee of the employer);

- Sex, race, creed, color, religion, national origin, or sexual orientation;

- Disabilities;

- National Guard or Reserve status;[10] and

- Date of military discharge.[11]

Employers should train interviewers and recruiters to ask appropriate questions. Interviewers also should be well informed about the Americans with Disabilities Act (discussed further in the Disability Discrimination section of this Guide) if that Act is applicable. Inappropriate questions include:

- Do you have any children? Do you intend to have any?

- How many children do you have? How old are they? Who will care for them while you are at work?

- If you become pregnant, will you quit your job?

- Do you use birth control?

- Are you married? What does your husband/wife think of all this?

- Whom can we contact in case of an emergency?[12]

- Have you ever tested HIV positive?

- What does your husband/wife do? Is your husband/wife a union member? How likely is it that your husband/wife will accept a job in another city?

- How does your husband/wife feel about you making more money than he/she does?

- How old are you?

- What year(s) did you graduate from (attend) high school? College?

- How would you feel about taking orders from someone younger than you?

- Have you ever been arrested?[13]

- Have you ever been treated for any of the following diseases or conditions?

- What languages are spoken in your home?

- Do you have a good credit rating? Have your wages ever been garnished?

- Do you have any physical impairments which would prevent you from performing the job for which you are applying?

- Are you now receiving or have you ever received workers' compensation benefits?

- How much do you weigh? How tall are you?

- What is the lowest salary you will accept?

- Do you smoke?

The Technical Assistance Manual on Title I of the Americans with Disabilities Act lists a number of additional prohibited questions,[14] including:

- Have you ever been hospitalized? If so, for what condition?

- Have you ever been treated by a psychiatrist or psychologist? If so, for what condition?

- Have you ever been treated for any mental condition?

- Is there any health-related reason you may not be able to perform the job for which you are applying?

- How many days were you absent from work because of illness last year?

- Are you taking any prescribed drugs?

- Have you ever been treated for drug addiction or alcoholism?

Interviewers and recruiters also should be trained to avoid making any notations on application forms. Codes, numbers or cryptic shorthand notes on the application could be misinterpreted. Such promises may impair the employer's right to terminate an individual. Interviewers should take detailed notes on a notepad separate from the application form and discard their notes after an applicant has been hired. Interviewers also should be trained to avoid making any oral or written representations to prospective candidates, e.g., "you'll have this job until you retire."

OUT OF TOWN AND RECRUITED CANDIDATES

Employers should be especially careful in their representations when recruiting someone who must move or is not actively seeking a change of employment. Detrimental reliance on such representations by an applicant who moves or quits an existing job can form the basis of an implied contract. In addition, it is unlawful for an employer to induce an individual to move within Minnesota, or from another state to Minnesota, based upon knowingly false representations concerning the kind or character of the work or the compensation paid. An employer who does so is guilty of a misdemeanor, and the employee is entitled to an action for damages.[15] Finally, legal counsel should be consulted regarding the existence of any industry specific statutory requirements. For example, Minnesota law requires employers in the food processing industry to provide written disclosure of the terms and conditions of employment to persons recruited to relocate. The statute allows civil actions and fines.[16]

AFFIRMATIVE ACTION

Before an individual is actually hired, a company that contracts with the government should consider what effect the hiring will have on its affirmative action obligations to recruit and advance qualified minorities, women, persons with disabilities and covered veterans. Federal, state and local laws each have different criteria for compliance with their respective affirmative action or equal employment opportunity requirements. Covered employers and federal, state and local criteria include:

- **Federal.** Each prime contractor or subcontractor that has 50 or more employees and a federal contract of $50,000 or more; or government bills of lading totaling $50,000 or more; or a depository of government funds; or issues U.S. savings bonds/notes, must develop a written affirmative action plan that covers minorities, women, persons with disabilities and covered veterans. Employers must implement the written affirmative action program, keep it on file and update it annually. The employer is also required to prepare the standard Form 100 (EEO-1), and a VETS-100 Reporting Form as well as satisfy other record-keeping obligations.[17] The EEO-1 and VETS-100 Forms must be filed annually by September 30th each year. The Department of Labor's Employment Standards Administrator's Office of Federal Contract Compliance Programs ("OFCCP") oversees federal affirmative action plans.

- **State.** In Minnesota, if an employer employed more than 40 full-time employees on a single working day during the previous 12 months and it holds or submits a bid or proposal for a state contract for goods or services in excess of $100,000, the employer is required to have a written affirmative action plan for the employment of qualified minority, female and disabled individuals.[18] The plan must be approved by the Commissioner of Human Rights, who then issues a Certificate of Compliance. This Certificate, which is a requirement for bidding on state contracts, is valid for two years. Covered employers must also submit an annual compliance report. The Department of Human Rights is responsible for enforcing compliance with this statute.

- **Local.** Minneapolis and St. Paul have city ordinances governing affirmative action requirements for contractors with the city.[19] Minneapolis requires contractors and subcontractors that do more than $50,000 of work with the city in a fiscal year to have a written affirmative action plan.[20] The Minneapolis Department of Civil Rights and the St. Paul Department of Human Rights enforce the respective city ordinances. Other cities may have similar ordinances.

Employers doing business with government entities or acting as subcontractors to businesses who contract with government entities should check with the entities involved and their own legal counsel concerning their affirmative action obligations.

BACKGROUND CHECKS

Employers hiring certain types of employees are required by law to perform background checks. For example, employers hiring security guards are required to check their backgrounds with the Bureau of Criminal Apprehension, and employers hiring certain counselors are required to check their references for evidence of sexual contact with patients or former patients.[21] Public and private schools are required to check the criminal history on all individuals who are offered employment in the school.[22] Rental property owners must request background information from the Bureau of Criminal Apprehension before hiring property managers.[23] Finally, employees, contractors and volunteers of a home health care provider or hospice are subject to background checks.[24]

In addition to the background checks required by statute, employers should perform background checks appropriate to the job for which the applicant is applying. For example, an employer hiring a convenience store clerk may want to conduct a background check because the clerk works primarily alone and handles cash.

The negligent hiring, retention and supervision doctrines also impose a duty on employers to use reasonable care in the selection, retention and supervision of employees. If an employer hires, retains or fails to supervise employees whom it knows or should know may cause harm, that duty has been breached and liability may result. In an effort to encourage employers to share important information about an employee's work history (when requested), Minnesota has a reference law designed to protect an employer from civil liability. A more complete discussion of Minnesota's reference law is discussed in the chapter on Terminations.

To avoid discrimination claims, an employer who performs background checks should be able to justify the inquiry. A hotel may want to conduct background checks on all of its employees who have access to guest rooms, as may a manufacturing company who hires employees to drive forklifts in the warehouse. Employers should not ask anything during a background check that cannot be asked of the applicant directly. Employers also need to be aware that outside firms used to conduct background checks must comply with these rules as well. Background checks should be done for all persons considered for the particular position as part of the hiring process.

Under the Americans with Disabilities Act, employers may ask an applicant's previous employers about job functions and tasks performed by the applicant, the quantity and quality of work performed, how job functions were done, the applicant's attendance record (not how many days the applicant was absent from work because of an illness or injury), and other job-related issues that do not relate to disability.[25]

Because the Minnesota Human Rights Act generally prohibits employers from seeking and obtaining information from any source that pertains to the individual's protected class (age, marital status, etc.) for the purpose of making a job decision, employers should exercise great caution and consult with counsel before obtaining background information.

Under the federal Fair Credit Reporting Act[26] and its Minnesota counterpart, the Access to Consumer Reports law,[27] Minnesota employers are subject to specific notification and disclosure requirements regarding their use of consumer credit reports to learn background information about applicants and employees.[28] Credit history checks may reveal marital status, date of birth or public assistance status. Employers are advised to consult legal counsel for a discussion of the rules and potential liabilities before they use these reports to assist them in their hiring and employment decisions.

PRE-EMPLOYMENT TESTING

This section discusses all pre-employment tests other than physical examinations and drug and alcohol tests. Under current law, a Minnesota employer may require an applicant to take a non-medical pre-employment test before the applicant receives a job offer. Such a pre-employment test must not be given for the purpose of discriminating against any protected class, and it also must meet the following criteria:

- The test must measure only essential job-related abilities.

- The test must be required of all applicants for the same position regardless of disability (except for tests authorized under workers' compensation law).

- The test must accurately measure the applicant's aptitude, achievement level or other relevant factors and may not reflect the applicant's impaired sensory, manual or speaking skills except when those skills are what is being tested.[29]

The above criteria also apply to employers subject to the Americans with Disabilities Act. If a pre-employment test tends to screen out individuals with disabilities on the basis of those disabilities, the ADA requires that the test be job-related and consistent with business necessity.

Employers testing applicants with impaired sensory, manual or speaking skills (when those skills are not what is being tested) must reasonably accommodate those applicants in the testing process. Such reasonable accommodation may mean, for example, giving an oral test to an individual with dyslexia or providing extra time to take a test to a person with a visual impairment or learning disability.

Employers who employ at least 15 employees during each of 20 or more calendar weeks in the current or preceding calendar year must also comply with the federal Equal Employment Opportunity Commission (EEOC) Guidelines for tests and other selection procedures which are used as a basis for any employment decision. Employment decisions include, but are not limited to, hiring, promotion, demotion, membership (for example, in a labor organization) referral and retention.[30] Under the EEOC Guidelines, an employer may be called upon to prove that its test does not discriminate on grounds of race, color, religion, sex or national origin. A selection rate for any race, sex, or ethnic group which is less than 80 percent of the selection rate for the group with the highest rate will generally be regarded by the federal enforcement agencies as evidence of adverse impact. The EEOC published an Enforcement Guidance on Employment Tests and

Selection Procedures in December 2007 that provides technical assistance on some common issues relating to federal anti-discrimination laws and the use of tests and other selection procedures in the employment process.

If the employer cannot show that its test has no adverse impact on protected groups, then it will be required to prove that its test is job-related and does not in fact discriminate. The methods of proof required at this point are beyond the scope of this Guide.

Any employer conducting a pre-employment test should be able to demonstrate that the test truly measures essential job-related abilities and individual characteristics. Unless the test is obviously job-related (i.e. to a layperson), such as a word processing test for an applicant applying for an administrative position, an employer may want to consult an expert familiar with the particular test under consideration to make sure that these standards are met. Reliance on expert advice may demonstrate an employer's good faith effort to comply with the requirements of the law.

Employers should not rely solely on pre-employment tests in making hiring decisions. Other hiring criteria should include the interview, relevant experience, education, availability, employment history and references.

An employer who conducts pre-employment tests should keep detailed records with regard to all testing and should monitor its hiring decisions based on the data which it accumulates. All test results should be kept strictly confidential.

All tests should be administered and scored in a nondiscriminatory manner. Tests should be given in the same environment for all applicants, and all applicants should be given the same equipment to perform the tests.

Timing an applicant's performance of a job-related task (e.g., typing) would be a non-medical test; however, measuring an applicant's physiological state–such as blood pressure or heart rate– following performance of the test, would likely constitute a medical or physical examination. Written tests which purport to test the honesty of the applicant and which do not measure physiological changes in the applicant are permitted under Minnesota law,[31] although courts in some other jurisdictions are showing disfavor toward "integrity" tests. Employers are generally prohibited from using lie detector (polygraph) tests on applicants or employees.[32]

PRE-EMPLOYMENT PHYSICAL EXAMINATIONS

MINNESOTA LAW

A Minnesota employer may require an applicant, as a condition of hire, to submit to a pre-employment physical exam, which may include a medical history, if:

- The applicant (except for certain peace officer applicants) has first received an offer of employment contingent only upon passing the physical;

- The physical examination tests only for essential job-related abilities; and

- The physical is required of all persons conditionally offered employment for the same position, regardless of disability (except for examinations authorized under Minnesota's workers' compensation law).[33]

The physical may include a drug or alcohol test if the requirements of the Minnesota drug testing statute (discussed below) are followed.

An employer may not refuse to employ an applicant due to physical inability to perform the job unless the applicant is unable to perform the essential functions of the job. Certain employers also have an obligation to explore whether they can "reasonably accommodate" the applicant to enable him or her to perform the essential functions of the job. "Reasonable accommodation" is required of any employer who employs 15 or more permanent full-time employees unless the employer can demonstrate that accommodation would impose an undue hardship on the company.[34] "Reasonable accommodation" means steps which must be taken to accommodate the known physical or mental limitations of a qualified disabled person.

An employer in Minnesota may ask an applicant whether he or she has a physical condition which could prevent the applicant from performing the job for which he or she is applying only as part of a pre-employment physical, after a conditional job offer has been made, and as part of the medical history which is part of that pre-employment physical. Note that all medical information must be collected and maintained on separate medical forms and in separate medical files, to be treated as confidential medical records, not as part of the employee's personnel file.

If the applicant undergoes a pre-employment physical and a physician determines that the applicant is unable to perform the job in question even with reasonable accommodation (if required), the employer must notify the applicant of that information within ten days of the final decision not to hire.[35]

Note that in addition to protecting applicants who actually have physical, mental or sensory impairments, Minnesota law also protects applicants who have a record of having such an impairment or who are perceived as having such an impairment against discrimination based on disability.

FEDERAL LAW

Under the Americans with Disabilities Act ("ADA"), consistent with Minnesota law, employers may not make any medical inquiries or submit applicants to any medical examinations before a conditional offer of employment is made, and the medical examination must be required of all persons conditionally offered employment for the same position. Unlike Minnesota law, under the ADA employers may perform medical examinations that are not job-related and may make unrestricted medical inquiries as long as the responses to those inquiries are not used to reject an applicant for reasons that are not job-related or consistent with business necessity. This approach, even though acceptable under the ADA, is not allowed under Minnesota law. Therefore, Minnesota employers should only perform medical examinations that test for job-related abilities.

DRUG AND ALCOHOL TESTING OF APPLICANTS

Minnesota employers may require a job applicant to undergo a drug and alcohol test if a job offer has been made to the applicant and the same test is required of all applicants conditionally offered employment for the same position.[36] The employer must have a written drug and alcohol testing policy which contains certain information required under Minnesota law. Each applicant should be given a copy of the policy, and notice of the existence and availability of the policy should be posted in appropriate and conspicuous workplace locations.

An applicant, before being tested, should first sign an acknowledgment that he or she has read the policy and understands that passing the drug and alcohol test is a requirement of the job. The applicant also has an opportunity, both before and after the testing, to list any prescription medications or any other explanation for a positive drug test. The applicant has other specific rights and the employer has specific responsibilities during the testing process. Testing must be done by a laboratory qualified by law to conduct testing, and there must be both an initial and confirmatory (second) drug test. If the confirmatory test is positive, the applicant may request a third test, to be conducted on the same sample at his or her own expense.

The employer must assure compliance with regulations published by the Minnesota Department of Health with respect to chain of custody and laboratory procedures, and it must assure that all drug testing information is kept strictly confidential.

An employer may withdraw a job offer if the applicant does not successfully pass the drug and alcohol screen. The employer must inform the applicant of the reason for the withdrawal within ten days of the decision not to hire.[37]

Note that different rules promulgated by the federal Department of Transportation ("DOT") apply to testing of job applicants who, for example, if hired, would operate a commercial motor vehicle or would possess a commercial driver's license in the course of their employment.[38] These rules may preempt state law. Discussion of the DOT drug and alcohol testing requirements for employees appears in the Drug Free Workplace Act and other Federal Requirements section of this Guide. Because these rules are complex, any employer in this situation is advised to consult with counsel on how to properly implement a testing program.

OFFER OF EMPLOYMENT

When offering employment to any individual, whether orally or by offer letter, the employer should be sure to avoid making statements such as "we look forward to a long and rewarding experience with you on our team." If the employer uses an offer letter, the terms and conditions of employment should be fully described as the company understands them, and the offer letter should indicate that it supersedes any oral promises. In addition, if the employer wants the employment relationship to be "at-will," that is, terminable by either party at any time, the letter should not include an annual salary; it should include a payroll period amount, e.g., weekly or semi-monthly, that is annualized at a rate of "X." This will insure that the offer is not construed to be for a one-year term. To insure that the offer letter will not be interpreted as a binding employment contract, the employer is advised to have the letter reviewed by legal counsel before it is sent.

NOTICE OF RIGHTS REGARDING PERSONNEL FILES

Although all Minnesota employers are required to provide employees with access to their personnel files,[39] employers with at least 20 employees should note that they must provide written notice to a job applicant upon hire of the new employee's rights and remedies regarding personnel records.[40] Employers are encouraged to secure a signed acknowledgment of the notice from each employee. Further discussion of personnel files appears in the Employee Access to Personnel Files section of this Guide.

IMMIGRATION LAW COMPLIANCE

Once an individual has been offered employment, the employer is required to verify that the individual is legally authorized to work in the United States.[41] The requirement of verification extends to all employees: lifetime U.S. residents as well as aliens. In other words, employers are not just required to verify individuals they perceive to be aliens. Individuals who are independent contractors do not need to complete a Form I-9. The law applies to all employers, regardless of the number of employees they have, and to all individuals hired after November 6, 1986.

The employer must attest on Form I-9, Employment Eligibility Verification, that it has examined documents establishing the following:

- The employee's authorization to work in this country ("work authorization"); and

- The employee's identity (in other words, an approved photo identification).

The employer does this by examining certain documents provided by the employee and specified on Form I-9. Specifically, the employer is required to examine either: (a) one document from those specified in Form I-9's "List A," or (b) one document from those specified in Form I-9's "List B" and one document from Form I-9's "List C." The employer may not specify which documents it will accept for verification. The employee can choose which document(s) the employee wants to present from the list of acceptable documents.

A new version of Form I-9 was issued in 2007. The significant revision to the 2007 Form I-9 is the removal of several "List A" documents that employers can accept to verify identity and employment eligibility. Employers may no longer accept the following five documents: Certificate of U.S. Citizenship (Form N-560 or N-561); Certificate of Naturalization (Form N-550 or N-570); the Alien Registration Receipt Card (Form I-151); the Reentry Permit (Form I-327); and the Refugee Travel Document (Form I-571). The 2007 Form I-9 also added the newest version of the Employment Authorization Document (EAD I-766) to the list of acceptable documents under "List A." The 2007 Form I-9 further provided that employees do not need to provide their Social Security number in Section 1 of Form I-9, unless they are employed by an employer who participates in the "E-Verify" program.

Effective April 3, 2009, employers will have to complete a new, revised I-9 form for all new hires and for reverification of certain employees with temporary work authorization. For the first time, the 2009 I-9 form requires new hires to distinguish between U.S. citizenship and non-citizen nationality. The 2009 I-9 form rules also prohibit employers from accepting expired documents to verify employment authorization. Previously, certain expired documents such as a U.S. passport were acceptable. Finally, the 2009 I-9 form reduces the number of acceptable documents that employers may accept to prove identity and employment authorization. Acceptable List A identity and employment authorization documentation will no longer include: Form I-688, Temporary Resident Card; Form I-688A, Employment Authorization Card; and Form 1688B, Employment Authorization Card. List A, however, will now include foreign passports containing certain machine-readable immigrant visas and passports from the Federated States of Micronesia and the Republic of the Marshall Islands if presented with an I-94 or I-94A arrival/departure record.

Employers must use the new 2009 Form I-9 for new employees and when re-verifying existing employees commencing on April 3, 2009. The new Form I-9 can be accessed at www.uscis.gov/files/form/I-9.pdf.

Section 1 of the Form I-9 must be completed by the employee at the time of hire.[42] For employees hired for more than three business days, Section 2 of the Form I-9 must be completed by the employer within three business days of the date the employee was hired. For employees hired for fewer than three business days, the form must be completed on the first day of employment.

If the employee is unable to provide the required verification documentation within three days of hire because a document is lost, stolen or damaged, the employee may present a receipt for the application for the verification document by the third day of employment.[43] The employee must present the actual document within 90 days of the date employment begins.[44] Form I-9 should be notated initially to reflect that a receipt was presented and later that the actual document was presented.

If the employee is an alien authorized to work until a specific date, the employer must re-verify the employee's employment eligibility on or before the date the employee's work authorization expires.[45] The employee must present a document that shows either an extension of the employee's initial employment authorization or new work authorization. Upon receipt of the documentation, the employer must complete Section 3 of the Form I-9 and record the new expiration date.

An employer can terminate an employee who:

(1) fails to produce the required documentation, or a receipt for a document, within three business days of the date employment begins;

(2) fails to produce the actual document within 90 days of the date employment begins, if the employee presented a receipt for a document within the first three business days of employment, or produces other work authorization; or

(3) fails to produce proof of current work authorization to continue to work when an employee's work authorization expires.

For more information on completing the Form I-9, employers can obtain the "Handbook for Employers-Instructions for Completing the Form I-9" (Immigration Form M-274), which can be obtained online from U.S. Citizenship and Immigration Services at www.uscis.gov/files/nativedocuments/m-274_3apr09.pdf.

Employers are required to retain all completed I-9 forms for either three years from the date of hiring or one year from the date the individual's employment is terminated, whichever is later.[46] Employers are permitted, but are not required, to copy the documents presented by the employee. If copies of those documents are retained, they must be kept together with the I-9 form. Employers should keep I-9 forms, however, separate from the employee's personnel record. The forms may be inspected by U.S. Immigration and Customs Enforcement and the U.S. Department of Labor.[47]

Unless an employer establishes a good faith defense, an employer that knowingly hires an unauthorized alien is liable for civil penalties of not less than $275 and not more than $2,200 for each unauthorized alien for the first violation occurring before March 27, 2008 and not less than $375 and not exceeding $3,200 for a first offense occurring after March 27, 2008; not less than $2,200 and not more than $5,500 for each unauthorized alien for the second violation occurring before March 27, 2008 and not less than $3,200 and not exceeding $5,500 for a second offense occurring after March 27, 2008; and not less than $3,300 and not more than $11,000 for each unauthorized alien for more than two violations occurring before March 27, 2008 and not less than $4,300 and not exceeding $16,000 for more than two offenses occurring after March 27, 2008.[48] Persons or employers convicted of engaging in a "pattern or practice" of hiring unauthorized aliens are subject to a fine of up to $3000 and/or imprisonment of up to six months for the entire pattern or practice.[49] "Pattern or practice" involves regular, repeated and intentional activities. Employers who fail to properly complete, retain and/or make available for inspection Forms I-9 as required by law may face civil money penalties of not less than $100 and not more than $1000 for each employee for whom such violation occurred.

A Minnesota executive order was recently passed requiring employers that are awarded state contracts in excess of $50,000 to certify their compliance with federal immigration laws and that they do not knowingly employ persons in violation of immigration laws.[50] Under the order, vendors and subcontractors must also certify that, as of the date state services will be performed, they have implemented or are in the process of implementing the federal government's "E-verify" program (an electronic employment verification system) for all newly hired employees in the United States. Employers that knowingly employ individuals who are ineligible to work risk having their contracts terminated and possibly being banned from doing business with the state.

The order also requires recipients of business subsidies to certify their compliance with federal immigration laws in relation to employees performing work in the United States.[51] The Commissioner of Economic Employment and Development is to establish the certification compliance procedures for these businesses.

An employer wishing to employ a foreign worker should be aware that there are a number of visa categories that allow an alien to work in the United States.

An alien who is an immigrant should have a Permanent Resident or Resident Alien card, more commonly known as a "Green Card." Generally, permanent residents may be employed by most U.S. employers.

In contrast, non-immigrant aliens are usually restricted to employment that has been approved and are limited to a specific employer. Some of the more common visa categories available to non-immigrant aliens are the H-1B; E-1 and E-2; L-1A and L-1B; and TN.

The H-1B category is available for specialty occupations that require a minimum of a bachelor's degree. The employer must demonstrate that it is offering the prevailing wage for the position in the employer's labor market and obtain an approved Labor Condition Application prior to petitioning to the Bureau of Immigration and Customs Enforcement to hire the alien. There is an annual "cap" on the number of H1-B petitions that the U.S. Citizenship and Immigration Services will approve each fiscal year (October 1 to September 30).

The E-l and E-2 categories are available to individuals who will commit a substantial investment in a U.S. enterprise. The investor must be a national of a "treaty" country as listed in the Department of State Foreign Affairs Manual. These categories are also available to certain executive, managerial, supervisory, or essential employees of the investor. Such employees must also have the nationality of the treaty country.

The L-1A and L-1B categories are available to intracompany transferees who are coming to the United States to work for a U.S. employer. The U.S. employer must have a qualifying business relationship with a foreign business entity, such as that of a parent company, subsidiary, joint venture, or branch office. The proposed employment must be in an executive or managerial capacity (L-1A) or for an employee with specialized knowledge of the business (L-1B).

The TN category, which was created as part of the North American Free Trade Agreement of 1994 (NAFTA), is available to employers that wish to employ Canadian or Mexican business professionals in one of the professions listed on NAFTA Schedule 2.[52]

There are also a number of other less-common visa categories and situations allowing an alien to work in the United States.

Employers should consult legal counsel with knowledge of immigration law if they are considering employing foreign immigrant or non-immigrant workers.

COURT-ORDERED OBLIGATIONS

INCOME WITHHOLDING FOR CHILD SUPPORT OR SPOUSAL MAINTENANCE

With respect to the payment of child support, medical support, maintenance and related payments, Minnesota employers are required to report certain information to the Minnesota Department of

Human Services on new employees and independent contractors, and on rehires, within twenty days of hiring the employee or engaging the independent contractor.[53]

Under this reporting system, employers must provide the Department of Human Services with the employee or independent contractor's name, address, social security number, and if available, date of birth. In addition, employers must provide their own name, address and federal employer identification number. The Department of Human Services has given employers different options for reporting such information, including mailing or faxing the person's W-4 form, or providing the information on a printed list, on magnetic tape, diskette, or via telephone (note that certain formatting requirements must be followed in some instances). For further information, contact the Department of Human Services at (651) 431-2000.

When the employee or independent contractor is required under order to pay child support, maintenance or related payments, the employer is required to begin withholding according to the terms of the order.[54] This obligation applies to wages or other lump sum payments made by the employer to the employee or independent contractor.

When the employer receives notice of court-ordered support, it must begin withholding no later than the first pay period that occurs after 14 days following the date of the notice.[55] The maximum amount which may be withheld for spousal maintenance or child support is 50 percent of the employee's disposable earnings if the employee is supporting a new spouse or another dependent child, and 60 percent if the employee is not supporting a spouse or other dependent child (55 and 65 percent respectively in certain cases where the employee is in arrears on court-ordered support or maintenance payments).[56] An employer may deduct $1 from the employee's remaining salary for each payment made pursuant to a withholding order in order to cover its expenses.[57]

DEPENDENT MEDICAL SUPPORT OBLIGATIONS

At the time of hire, an individual (whether an employee or independent contractor) is required to disclose whether medical support is required to be withheld from his or her pay.[58] If so, employers are required to withhold such amounts in the same manner as amounts for child support, maintenance or related payments. Employers must request that new employees disclose whether they have been ordered by a court to provide health and dental dependent insurance coverage. If a new employee discloses an obligation to obtain health and dental dependent insurance coverage and coverage is available through the employer, the employer is required to make all application processes known to the employee upon hiring, and to enroll the new employee and dependent in the plan. An employer or union that willfully fails to comply with the court order is liable for any health or dental expenses incurred by the dependents during the period of time the dependents were eligible to be enrolled in the insurance program, and for any other premium costs incurred because the employer or the union willfully failed to follow the court order. The employer can also be required to pay a fine of $500, and can be held in contempt of court.

NON-COMPETITION AGREEMENTS, NON-SOLICITATION AGREEMENTS, AND INTELLECTUAL PROPERTY RIGHTS

In a world of global trade and instantaneous communication, the best investment a business can make may be in intellectual capital, and its greatest source of wealth may be knowledge. Intellectual capital is likely to be developed by employees paid to think and to apply their ingenuity and talents for the benefit of employers. To protect its intellectual capital, a business must secure its copyrights, patents, trade secrets, trademarks, service marks, and trade names. The first step in that process is the employer entering into a formal agreement with each employee that clearly establishes that the employer owns and retains control of the intellectual capital, even after the employee has moved on to a new job at a different company, or even when the employee has become a competitor.

Employment contracts and independent contractor agreements are critical to securing a business's intellectual property. Appropriate contract language is essential for an employer who seeks to limit the damage caused when its intellectual property rights have been misappropriated by former employees or independent contractors. Employers also may rely on statutory and common law protection, but well-crafted agreements are the best protection.

NON-COMPETITION AND NON-SOLICITATION AGREEMENTS

As a condition of employment, an employer may require that an applicant or employee sign an agreement not to work for a competitor and not to form a competing business during the term of his or her employment or after he or she departs. The agreement also may provide that the individual may not solicit the employer's customers or employees when he or she starts a competing business or works for another employer. Confidentiality obligations are almost always included in non-compete agreements; agreements to assign inventions may also be included. Such agreements are enforceable against former employees and independent contractors if they protect a legitimate interest of the employer, are supported by adequate consideration, and are reasonably limited in scope and in time.[59] Non-competition and non-solicitation agreements should be separate documents, distinct from other employment paperwork. If the employee is employed "at will," the non-compete agreement should state specifically that it is a separate agreement to protect intellectual property rights, not an employment contract, and that it does not modify what otherwise may be an "at will" employment relationship.

Adequate consideration for a covenant not to compete varies from case to case. Courts generally agree that consideration is adequate when, for example, the agreement was executed as a condition of, and in consideration of, hiring, or in exchange for payment. If an employer is going to require a new employee to sign a non-competition or non-solicitation agreement, the employer should provide notice to the prospective employee at the time the offer of employment is made, so that the new employee knows that he or she will be expected to sign the agreement as a condition of hire. Ideally, the prospective employee will receive notice before he or she has quit another job, moved to a new location, or otherwise made changes in his or her life in reliance on his or her expectation of new employment. Because there is no such thing as a "standard" non-competition agreement, an employer should provide a prospective employee with an opportunity to review and respond to the proposed agreement before he or she accepts the new job. If an employee has verbally accepted an offer of employment without being advised that such an agreement will be required, or without an opportunity to review the terms, the agreement may have to be supported by separate consideration, such as a cash payment, in addition to the initial offer of employment.

Employers should review non-competition/non-solicitation/confidentiality agreements with existing employees to determine if each agreement was adequately supported by consideration at the time it was signed. If there is a question about the fact of or adequacy of consideration, the agreement may not be enforceable unless the employee signs a new agreement promising not to compete and receives new consideration.

Because the law generally disfavors non-compete agreements, it is important that the language in each contract be appropriately drafted to protect the specific interest of the employer in each circumstance. Courts determine if restrictions are reasonable in scope and time based on their evaluations of individual contracts. For example, a non-compete agreement executed by the seller as part of the sale of a business is likely to be enforceable for a decade or longer.[60] In the employment context, by contrast, restrictive covenants may endure for two or at most three years. Because courts view covenants not to compete with skepticism, the contract may be interpreted against the employer. For example, a non-compete covenant in an employment contract may not be enforceable after an employee has been fired unless it is absolutely clear that the parties intended the non-compete clause to survive even involuntary termination of employment.[61]

Where restrictions are determined to be overly broad, a court may modify or "blue pencil" the agreement by substituting reasonable geographical scope and time limitations.[62] In egregious cases of employer overreaching, courts will refuse to enforce an unreasonable agreement at all. Some states, like Wisconsin, do not permit a court to "blue pencil" an agreement. Instead, Wisconsin courts will simply declare such a contract invalid and unenforceable if even a single provision is deemed to be overbroad. Some states also may refuse to enforce an agreement by one of their residents, even if the agreement selects the law of another jurisdiction; no matter what law the parties have agreed will apply, the courts of these states will apply their own state law, which may have the effect of invalidating the agreement. A Minnesota employer must take care to ensure that non-competition agreements comply with the laws of the states where its employees live. If an employee lives in North Dakota, for example, the non-competition agreement may not be enforceable at all if the court applies the law of the employee's state of residence. If a court applies South Dakota law, the non-compete may be enforced for a maximum of two years, and possibly not at all. Thus, an employer with employees located in several states should carefully tailor the non-compete agreement for each employee to ensure that it is enforceable wherever the employee lives, regardless of what law is applied.

Before an offer of employment is made, employers also should determine if a prospective employee is subject to a non-competition, non-solicitation or confidentiality agreement with a prior employer that may restrict or limit that applicant's ability to perform effectively. An employer who hires a new employee without making such an inquiry may be liable for interference with the previous contract of employment and could be ordered to pay the previous employer damages, including attorney fees.[63]

Non-competition agreements do not automatically establish ownership of intellectual property and cannot prevent all forms of direct and indirect competitive damage by former employees if they have had access to valuable intellectual property. Such intellectual property may be transferred overtly or covertly to a third party without technically violating the non-compete provision.

By establishing at the outset its ownership of intellectual property, an employer may establish that the employee, ex-employee, or independent contractor has no right to certain copyrights, patents, trade secrets, or trademarks, regardless of whether that individual is subject to an enforceable non-compete agreement. If properly drafted, an assignment contract will convey those rights to the employer and prevent misappropriation.

COPYRIGHTS

To be protected under the federal Copyright Act, a work must be an original work of authorship, fixed in any tangible medium of expression now known or later developed, from which the work can be perceived, reproduced, or otherwise communicated, with or without the aid of a machine or device.[64] The phase, "original work of authorship" does not require "novelty, ingenuity, or aesthetic merit."[65] The work must, however, "possess at least some minimal degree of creativity."[66] Works subject to copyright include literary works, musical works, and dramatic works; pantomimes and choreographic works; pictorial, graphic and sculptural works; motion pictures and other audiovisual works; and sound recordings and architectural works. [67]

The presumed owner of a copyright is the party that actually creates the work. In an employer-employee relationship, the employer is presumed to be the "author" of copyrightable works created by its employees acting within the scope of their employment.[68] The employer, not the employee, owns the intellectual property that the employees create on the job.[69]

Only works created by an employee "within the scope of employment" automatically become the property of the employer, however. The conduct of an employee is considered within the scope of employment if: (1) it is the kind of work the employee is employed to perform; (2) the employee creates the work substantially within authorized time and space limits; and (3) the work is motivated at least in part by a purpose to serve the employer.[70] Most courts require an employer to prove all three elements to establish its right to copyright ownership.

A carefully drafted written agreement between the employer and the employee should confirm that the employer owns the copyright; that is, that the employee created the work within the scope of his or her employment and that the employer is, as provided by law, considered the author. An agreement also should assign to the employer a copyright in any works created by the employee during the period of his or her employment. After receiving an executed assignment, the employer still is in a position to claim ownership of the copyright, even if the employee disputes the existence of one or more of the three elements necessary to show that the work was made "within the scope of employment."

In an independent contractor relationship, the independent contractor is presumed to be the author of the work and the owner of the copyright unless the work was created pursuant to a written "work made for hire" agreement[71] or is subsequently assigned to the employer.[72] An individual who performs regular work for the same employer at the same location nonetheless may be an independent contractor rather than an employee, if, for example, the employer does not withhold income taxes or Social Security benefits from payments or declines to extend benefits such as medical insurance.[73] If the individuals who create a work may be independent contractors or employees acting outside the scope of their employment, the employer must obtain an assignment of the copyright and all rights therein. To avoid any ambiguity as to ownership, an employer should routinely require all employees and independent contractors who are in a position to create copyrightable works to execute copyright assignment agreements both before and after completion of the work.

Fulfilling the requirement of a written assignment is crucial if the author is an independent contractor. The only works eligible for "work made for hire" treatment outside of the employment context are those that fall under one of nine specific categories enumerated in the federal Copyright Act as "works made for hire."[74] In those nine categories, a work may be a "work made for hire" if (and only if) the parties have expressly agreed in writing that the commissioning party (the employer), not the independent contractor, is the author.[75]

An employer and an independent contractor cannot by agreement transform a work into one "made for hire" unless the work falls into one of the nine statutory categories. Therefore, contractual language that states that the work of an independent contractor is a "work made for hire" may be an ineffective transfer of the copyright. In that case, the independent contractor, not the employer, may retain copyright ownership. It is less important for the employer to obtain an agreement designating the work as one "made for hire" than it is for the employer to obtain an unequivocal assignment of ownership.

PATENTS

Although rules of ownership applicable to copyrighted works are established by statute under the federal Copyright Act, ownership of inventions is generally governed by applicable state law, which may vary from jurisdiction to jurisdiction. Absent an agreement to the contrary, the law vests ownership of inventions in the inventing party, whether that party is an employee or an independent contractor. This may be true even if the employer paid for the invention or otherwise had some expectation of ownership. Thus, carefully drafted written documents assigning to the employer inventions created by both employees and independent contractors are essential to protect an employer's intellectual property.

Given the general rule applicable to traditional employment relationships, it is not surprising that independent contractors are in an even stronger position to assert ownership of their inventions in the absence of an express agreement to the contrary. Thus, employers should start with the presumption that, unless there is an agreement to the contrary, employees, consultants, and independent contractors own the inventions they have created. The employer must obtain an assignment in almost every situation.

Despite the general rule vesting ownership of inventions in both employees and independent contractors, employers may obtain rights to these inventions by receiving an express assignment of ownership in the invention. Employers also may obtain ownership under the "hired to invent" doctrine or the "shop rights" doctrine, and when the employer obtains an express assignment of ownership in the invention. To obtain patent rights by any of these means, an employer must take affirmative steps to protect its interest in intellectual property. Note also that, as explained further below, employers may obtain rights to the inventions of certain of its officers, directors and agents under a "fiduciary duty" analysis.

Under the traditional "hired to invent" rule, if an employee is initially hired or later directed to invent or attempt to invent a particular invention, the employer is entitled to ownership of resulting patents.[76] The absence of an express agreement will not always prevent an employer from successfully asserting patent rights, however. An implied-in-fact contract may arise between an inventor and his employer, where the employee was required by the employer to work on a particular project and used the employer's resources to develop the invention in dispute. This is particularly true if there were co-inventors who were other employees of the employer, and where the employer paid for a patent application.

Courts are generally reluctant to apply the "hired to invent" doctrine if the employee was not in fact hired to invent or was retained only to perform general research functions. An employee also may retain ownership of an invention when he or she has been hired to create a specific invention but later creates a different invention outside his or her assigned duties. The "hired to invent" doctrine is most typically applied in the context of traditional employer-employee relationships, and courts are reluctant to apply the rule to independent contractors.

In addition to the "hired to invent" doctrine, courts have recognized the "shop rights" doctrine under which employers may be entitled to limited rights in an employee's invention based on the particular facts of the case. Under the "shop rights" doctrine, the actions of an employer and employee may lead to the assumption that the employee accepted the employer's assistance in exchange for granting the employer limited future use of an invention, i.e., an "implied-in-fact" license.[77] When an employee, through words or silence, action or inaction, induces an employer to rely on the use of an invention, the employee cannot later deny the employer a right to use the invention, or seek additional compensation. For example, an employee who invented a device useful in retail display of merchandise and who persuaded her employer to demonstrate that device in retail stores would be prohibited, after obtaining a patent, from demanding a license fee from that employer for future use.

Regardless of its application to employees and independent contractors, the limited doctrine of "shop rights" does not vest actual ownership of patent rights in an employer. Instead, those rights will be held by the inventor and licensed, free of charge, to the employer. The employer may not assign or otherwise transfer its limited "shop rights" to a third party. An express assignment of rights is clearly superior to obtaining a limited interest by application of the "shop rights" doctrine.

Patent rights also may devolve to the employer when a special trust relationship is present with the inventor. Essentially, this rule is based on the notion that certain employees, typically corporate officers and directors, owe a fiduciary duty to the employer preventing them from competing with the employer or usurping "corporate opportunities."[78] The fiduciary duty analysis is helpful in preventing influential employees from abusing their position to the detriment of a corporation, but the doctrine is of limited utility because it applies only to certain officers, directors and agents.

The favored method by which an employer acquires employee inventions is to enter into an express contract with the employee or independent contractor. By statute, an employment agreement cannot require an employee to assign, or offer to assign, an employee's invention to the employer if no equipment, supplies, facilities, or trade secret information of the employer is used to create the invention and the invention is developed entirely on the employee's own time.[79] The employee is entitled to this protection by law, provided that the invention does not result from any work performed for the employer, or does not relate directly to the employer's business or to its actual or demonstratively anticipated research or development. An employment contract provision forcing the inventor to assign an unrelated invention is void and unenforceable. In addition, an employer cannot require that the employee assign such an invention as a condition of employment or continuing employment (of course, nothing prohibits the employer from negotiating for an assignment from an employee in exchange for valid consideration, such as a cash payment). Finally, an employment agreement that contains an invention assignment provision also must provide written notification to the employee that the agreement does not apply to inventions created outside the scope of employment.[80]

Employers also must be cautious about exposing new inventions to employees. Under the federal Patent Act,[81] an inventor forfeits patent protection if the invention is in public use for more than one year before the patent application is filed.[82] Public use even may mean in-house testing among employees, if it takes place more than a year before the patent application is filed and other precautions have not been taken.[83] To guard against forfeiting potentially valuable patent rights by testing inventions with employees, an employer must maintain strict secrecy requirements, confirm in writing the secrecy obligation of each employee, maintain an experimental atmosphere, and limit the experiment to claims in the patent.

TRADE SECRETS

The Uniform Trade Secrets Act, adopted by Minnesota, defines a trade secret as "information" that:

a) derives independent economic value, actual or potential, from not being generally known to, and not being readily ascertainable by proper means by, other persons who can obtain economic value from its disclosure or use; and

b) is the subject of efforts that are reasonable under the circumstances to maintain its secrecy.[84]

Trade secrets may be unique principles, engineering logic, coherence and computer software, but they also may be customer lists and marketing information. A trade secret may modify and improve standard models to such an extent that a newer version becomes unique in the industry. Generally known information may gain trade secret protection because of a peculiar combination of data. If the exact combination of certain features is unique, even though none of the processes or features is unique in an industry, and exact combinations are the only way to achieve the required performance, a trade secret may exist. Several competitors with the same information hypothetically each could own trade secret rights in the same information, if each maintained the appropriate protections.

It is difficult to prevent an employee from discovering trade secrets, particularly if that employee is among the group who developed the secret. However, an employer can take many precautions to protect its trade secrets from disclosure. They include restricting physical or computer access to sensitive areas; physical protection, such as security guards, personnel badges and restricted access areas; restricting copying and dissemination of sensitive information; putting employees "on notice" of trade secrets by marking documents or computer files as "secret" or "confidential;" requiring that only employees who "need to know" have access to secrets; and obtaining confidentiality agreements from the employees who have access to trade secret information.

An employer's efforts to maintain the secrecy of information need not be perfect, but its measures must be reasonable under the circumstances. The employer's systematic use of confidentiality agreements is particularly valuable. An employer should require most, if not all, employees to execute agreements acknowledging that the company owns trade secrets and promising never to disclose them, either during employment or after termination. Such an agreement (1) confirms that the employee is aware of a duty to maintain secrecy; (2) refutes any claim the employee may assert to ownership; and (3) puts the employee in a difficult position–he or she cannot, without contradicting an earlier signed statement, claim that what was once acknowledged as a secret is now publicly known or independently created. Moreover, the use of such an agreement will help an employer to demonstrate that it took "reasonable steps" to maintain the confidentiality of its trade secrets, a prerequisite to protection under the Uniform Trade Secrets Act.

The Computer Fraud and Abuse Act ("CFAA")[85] may provide employers with additional protection against employees or former employees who unlawfully access company computers to copy or transmit proprietary information directly or indirectly to themselves or to new employers. Although the courts have offered differing interpretations of the CFAA,[86] the statute may provides a mechanism for obtaining an injunction, damages, and attorney fees against anyone, including a former or soon-to-be-departing employee, who uses the employer's computers to loot trade secrets or other valuable intellectual property.

TRADEMARKS AND SERVICE MARKS

An employee or independent contractor who conceives of a successful trademark or trade name may conclude that the mark is personal, not employer, property. As a matter of law, however, if the employer has used the mark, the employee has little or no claim to ownership of it. Unlike patent law, rights in trademarks and service marks are not gained through discovery or invention, but only through actual use.[87] The person who first conceives the idea of using a given symbol as a mark does not automatically receive trademark priority. An employer who uses a mark conceived by an employee, or a client who uses a mark conceived by an independent contractor such as an advertising agency, ordinarily acquires the trademark rights.

In some cases, however, an employee or independent contractor who, by contract, establishes ownership of trademarks, ideas or concepts will be able to take them with her when he or she departs, depriving the employer of its investment in the good will attached to the trademark.[88] For complete protection, an employer should require each employee or independent contractor to assign in writing any trademark rights in marks or titles that he or she has created.

WAGE AND HOUR ISSUES

FAIR LABOR STANDARDS ACT COVERAGE

Employers must pay minimum wages and overtime pay to certain employees for hours worked. What the minimum wage is, when overtime is to be paid, who is a covered employee, and what constitutes hours worked, however, varies between state and federal law. Because the federal Fair Labor Standards Act ("FLSA") covers employees of enterprises whose workers are engaged in interstate commerce, or handle, sell or otherwise work on goods or materials that have been moved in or produced for interstate commerce, most employers and their employees in Minnesota are governed by the federal FLSA. Therefore, employers should assume that their business is covered by the federal FLSA unless the employer has been advised otherwise by its legal counsel. Even if the employer assumes that its business is covered under the federal FLSA, the employer still needs to be aware of Minnesota's provisions if such provisions are more favorable to the employee.

MINIMUM WAGE

The minimum wage for non-exempt employees of federally-covered employers is currently $6.55 per hour.[89] The minimum wage for non-exempt employees of state-covered large employers is currently $6.15 per hour.[90] The minimum wage for non-exempt employees of state-covered small employers (those with gross annual sales less than $625,000) and certain employees (i.e., sheltered workers, trainees) is $5.25 per hour.[91] Employers should note, however, that state and federal minimum wage requirements may be subject to increase. Minimum wage provisions apply to part-time employees.[92] The minimum wage law for both federal-covered and state-covered employers also provides that during the first 90 consecutive days of employment, an employer may pay an employee under the age of 20 years an "opportunity" wage. The minimum wage for these federal-covered employees is currently $4.25 per hour and $4.90 per hour for state-covered employees. Employers may not take any action to displace an employee in order to hire an employee at this lower rate.[93]

TIP CREDITS

There are no "tip credits" in Minnesota.[94] Employers must pay minimum wage even to employees who earn tips. Further, employers may not require employees to contribute or share gratuities received with the employer or other employees or to contribute any or all of their gratuities to a fund or pool operated for the benefit of the employer or employees. Employees may voluntarily share their gratuities with other employees, if the agreement to do so is made without employer participation.[95]

DEDUCTIONS FROM WAGES

Employers may only deduct certain items from an employee's wages. If the employee makes the proper written authorization, the employer may make the following deductions:

- Union dues

- Premiums for:

    - Life insurance
    - Hospitalization and surgical insurance
    - Group accident and health insurance
    - Group term life insurance
    - Group annuities

- Contributions to:

    - Credit unions or a community chest fund
    - A local arts and science council or a local science council
    - Minnesota benefit association
    - A federally or state registered political action committee

- Participation in an employee stock purchase plan or savings plan for periods longer than 60 days.[96]

No deductions may be made for the following items if the deduction would reduce an employee's wages below minimum wage, or if the deduction exceeds $50.00:

- Purchased or rented uniforms or specially designed clothing required by the employer, by the nature of the employment, or by law, which is not generally appropriate for use except in that employment;

- Purchased or rented equipment used in employment, except tools of a trade, a motor vehicle, or any other equipment which may be used outside the employment;

- Consumable supplies required in the course of that employment; and

- Travel expenses incurred in the course of employment except those incurred in traveling to and from the employee's residence and place of employment.[97]

When the employee's employment is terminated, the employer must reimburse the full amount deducted for any of the items listed above. When reimbursement is made, the employer may require the employee to surrender any existing items for which the employer provided reimbursement. The employer may not, however, hold the employee's final check if the employee fails to return such items.

An employer may not deduct from wages due or earned by an employee any amount for lost, stolen or damaged property, or recover any claimed amount owed by the employee to the employer, unless the employee voluntarily authorizes the employer in writing to make the deduction *after the loss has occurred*, or unless the employee is found liable by a court for the loss or indebtedness.[98] Wage assignments for married employees require spousal written consent.

Any written authorization must set forth the amount to be deducted from the employee's wages during each pay period. There are specific statutory limits on the amount which may be deducted in each pay period.

The prohibitions on wage deductions do not apply to:

- Independent contractors;

- Cases where a contrary provision in a collective bargaining agreement exists;

- Employees who are commissioned sales people, where the rules are established for purposes of discipline, or where the employee has committed errors or omissions in performing his or her duties; or

- Cases where an employee, prior to making a purchase or taking a loan from the employer, authorizes in writing that the cost of the purchase or loan shall be deducted from the employee's wages at certain intervals, or upon termination of employment.

HOURS WORKED

Minimum wage must be paid to non-exempt employees for all hours worked. Hours worked include training time, on-call time, cleaning time, waiting time, or any other time when the employee must be either on the premises of the employer or involved in the performance of duties in connection with his or her employment or must remain on the premises until work is prepared or available.[99] Hours worked do not include days on which the employee does not perform any work, such as paid holidays, vacation, sick leave, or other paid time off. Employees and employers may not agree to work "off the clock."

Periods when the employee is completely relieved of duty and free to leave the premises for a definite period of time, and the period is long enough for the employee to use for the employee's own purposes, are not hours worked.[100] An employee is not completely relieved of duty unless he or she is definitely told ahead of time that he or she will not have to commence work until a specified hour has arrived and that he or she may leave the job until that time.

Special rules apply for certain occupations, such as bus and truck drivers, emergency personnel, personal care attendants or live-in companions. Employers should be aware of exceptions specific to their industry.

ON-CALL TIME

Employees who are required to remain on call on the employer's premises or so close that they cannot use the time effectively for their own purposes are working while "on call." Employees who are not required to remain on the employer's premises but are merely required to carry a pager or leave word where they may be reached probably are not working while "on call."[101] The mere fact of being "on call" under these circumstances does not require pay. If an employee is working while "on call," he or she must be paid for that time. Employers should review on-call restrictions with legal counsel to determine whether the restrictions on the employee's time are significant enough to be considered working time.

SLEEPING TIME AS HOURS WORKED

If an employee is required to be on duty for 24 hours or more, bona fide meal periods and a bona fide regularly scheduled sleeping schedule of not more than eight hours may be excluded from hours worked upon agreement between the employer and employee if adequate sleeping facilities are furnished by the employer and the employee can usually enjoy an uninterrupted sleeping period. If the employee sleeps more than eight hours, only eight hours will be excluded from hours worked. If a sleeping period is interrupted by a call to duty, the interruption must be counted as hours worked. If the employee cannot get a minimum of five hours of sleep as the result of interruptions, the entire period must be counted as hours worked.

If the employer does not have an agreement with the employee regarding exclusion of meal periods and sleeping periods, meal periods and up to eight hours of sleeping time will constitute hours worked.[102] Minnesota law is more restrictive than federal law in this area, and special rules apply for various occupations.

MEALS

Employers must permit employees who work for eight or more consecutive hours sufficient time to eat a meal, but they are not required to pay employees for this time.[103] Meal periods of less than 20 minutes may not be deducted from hours worked, and meal periods may not be deducted where an employee is not entirely free from work responsibility, e.g., where an office employee is required to eat at his or her desk or a factory worker is required to be at his or her machine.[104] If an employee prefers to skip the designated meal period and continue working instead, it is the employer's decision whether to permit the employee to do so. An employer is not required to permit employees to accumulate break or meal time to alter their work schedule. However, the employee must be compensated for all hours worked.

If an employer serves the employee a meal and the employee accepts it, the employer receives credit toward the minimum wage for 60 percent of one hour's wage per meal at the adult minimum wage rate.[105] The employer, however, may not require the employee to accept meals as a condition of employment. To qualify for this meal allowance, the meal must include one food from each of the following four groups: fruits or vegetables; cereals, bread or potatoes; eggs, meat or fish; and milk, tea or coffee. For breakfast meals, eggs, meat or fish do not need to be included if both cereal and bread are offered.

BREAKS

Generally, employers are not required by law to give breaks of a specific duration. However, employers must allow employees adequate time within each four consecutive hours of work to use the restroom.[106] Such breaks are considered working time. An employer must provide reasonable unpaid break time for nursing mothers to express breast milk for their infant children. Employers must provide a lockable private facility, other than a toilet stall, for such purposes.[107]

TRAVEL

Travel time from home to work is not considered hours worked for which an employee must be compensated.

Time spent traveling by an employee during his or her normal work day must be counted as hours worked, as must travel time on non-working days that falls within the hours the employee usually works. If an employee finishes his or her job at an off-site location and, instead of returning to the regular job site, returns home, that travel time would not be counted as hours worked. Travel time spent during a time of day other than the employee's regular working hours as a passenger on an airplane, train, boat, bus or automobile to a place away from the employee's home community will not be considered work time unless the employee is required to work while traveling.[108]

OVERTIME PAY

Federally-covered employers must pay non-exempt employees overtime at one and one half times their regular rate of pay for work performed in excess of 40 hours per week.[109] State-covered employers must pay non-exempt employees overtime at one and one half times their regular rate for work performed in excess of 48 hours in a week.[110] "Non-exempt" employees are those employees covered by state or federal wage and hour laws. "Exempt" employees, as defined in the following section, are not subject to these laws. Special exceptions may apply for health care employees and certain other limited occupations.[111] There is no statutory requirement for overtime pay on weekends, holidays or after 8 hours. However, collective bargaining agreements or employer policies may permit such payment.

COMPENSATORY TIME OFF (COMP TIME)

"Comp time" (compensatory time off) generally means time off in lieu of time and a half pay for hours over 40 worked in a *workweek*, not a "pay period," by a non-exempt employee. "Comp time" is not permitted for private employees, only public employees.

EMPLOYEES EXEMPT FROM MINIMUM WAGE AND OVERTIME PROVISIONS

Individuals employed in bona fide executive, administrative, professional or outside sales positions and who are paid on a salary basis, are exempt from the minimum wage and overtime provisions of the federal FLSA. In Minnesota, executives, administrators, professionals and outside salespersons also are not subject to minimum wage and overtime provisions because they are excluded from the definition of "employees" in Minnesota's FLSA. Each type of position—executive, administrative, professional, computer professional and outside sales—has a test which is used to determine whether an individual worker fits a particular exemption. Because the regulations governing this area are extensive, employers should consult with their legal counsel before treating an individual employee as exempt.[112] Should the employer mis-classify an employee, the penalty may include unpaid overtime for that employee and other similarly classified employees for at least the past two years.

Employers are encouraged to review the new tests under the FLSA at www.dol.gov for specific salary and duties requirements of exempt employees.

An employee can be paid a salary and still not be an exempt employee because he or she does not fit one of the above exemptions. An employee who is paid on an hourly basis rather than a salary basis generally cannot be an exempt employee. An exception to this rule exists for computer professionals if their hourly rate of pay is at least $27.63 per hour.[113]

The primary duties of the employee (not just the job title) determine his or her status as an exempt or non-exempt employee.[114] Only where the employee's primary duties meet all the criteria under a particular test may the employee be exempt from the minimum wage and overtime provisions of the federal and state FLSAs.[115] Regardless of duties, employees earning less than $23,660 or generally classified as "blue collar" employees must receive overtime pay.[116]

Both professionals and administrators, in order to be exempt, must exercise discretion. The exercise of discretion is not meant to include those day-to-day decisions which, although they are necessary to the daily operations of the business, are routine, or involve prescribed procedures or a determination of whether specific standards are met, or are lacking in substantial importance to the employer's business as a whole. Certain employees who receive total annual compensation of at least $100,000 may be exempt if they customarily perform exempt duties.[117]

Exempt employees are generally required to be paid a guaranteed salary for a workweek in which any hours are worked[118] and deductions from that salary may only be made under very limited circumstances.[119] Deductions from pay may not be made for partial day absences, except as permitted under the Family and Medical Leave Act.[120] However, employers may require employees to deduct time for established PTO, vacation or sick leave accruals. Additional pay, usually on a regular basis and according to a formula or system, may appear to constitute overtime pay, inconsistent with the concept of "salary basis," in the view of some courts. Compensation systems for exempt employees that involve either deductions from or additions to salary should be carefully reviewed by legal counsel. Impermissible payment programs may destroy the FLSA exemption for any employee potentially subject to such a payment program.

WORK HOURS FOR MINORS

Minors, under the wage and hour laws, are those individuals who have not yet attained age 18. There is quite a disparity between federal and state laws in this area of law and employers are encouraged to consult legal counsel. Minors under 14 are not permitted to work in Minnesota except in limited occupations (babysitting, newspaper delivery, agricultural operations, youth athletic referees, etc.).[121] Minors under 16 may not work before 7 a.m. or after 9 p.m. on any day. They may not work more than 8 hours per day or 40 hours in a week. High school students under age 18 are restricted from working after 11 p.m. the night before a school day and before 5 a.m. on a school day subject to limited exceptions. If the minor age 16 or 17 obtains a note of permission from a parent or a guardian, the student may be permitted to work until 11:30 p.m. before a school day and begin at 4:30 a.m. on a school day.[122] Both federal and state law have unique restrictions that should be carefully reviewed. Employment certificates may be obtained to permit limited exceptions.

Certain types of employment may be prohibited completely for minors under 16, or severely restricted for minors under 18. When an employer seeks to hire a minor, legal counsel should be consulted concerning whether the minor can legally perform the job in question.[123]

AGE CERTIFICATES

Employers must require minors to provide proof of age through a copy of the minor's age certificate, birth certificate, copy of the minor's driver's license, or a Form I-9.[124] Employers also may rely upon state or federal age certificates for their minor employees, usually completed by the minor's school. The age certificate ensures that the minor is in fact the age he represents himself to be, and the employer is entitled to rely upon this certification. Age certificates, therefore, protect employers from unwitting violation of child labor laws.[125] Employers are subject to minimum wage and overtime laws and penalties for the employment of minors and to specific additional penalties for violations of the child labor laws.[126] Caution: disparities exist between federal and state child labor laws. Employers should check all applicable laws.

PAYMENT OF WAGES TO CURRENT EMPLOYEES

Employers must pay transitory employees and employees whose work requires the employee to change his or her place of residence, at intervals of not more than 15 days.[127] All other employees must be paid at least once every 31 days on a regular pay day designated in advance by the employer.[128] If wages due are not paid, the Commissioner of Labor and Industry may demand payment on behalf of the employee.[129] If wages are not paid within 10 days of the Commissioner's demand, the Commissioner may charge and collect the wages due and assess a penalty of up to 15 days' wages. Employers should consult legal counsel if any difficulties with respect to payment of employee wages arise. Employees may not be paid in non-negotiable instruments (scrip, options, etc.). Direct deposit of payroll checks cannot be mandatory, except for employees of municipalities.[130]

COMMISSIONER OF LABOR AND INDUSTRY

The Commissioner of Labor and Industry is chief of the Division of Labor Standards in the Department of Labor and Industry. The Commissioner may inspect all employer records that pertain to wages, hours and other conditions of employment. The Commissioner is also empowered to investigate wage complaints against employers. If the records maintained by the employer do not provide sufficient information to determine the exact amount of back wages due to an employee, the Commissioner may make a determination of wages due based upon the available evidence. Failure to submit records may subject the employer to fines and penalties.[131]

With respect to violations of certain statutes or rules, the Commissioner shall issue cease and desist orders, shall take whatever steps he or she determines necessary to effectuate the purposes of the rule or statute violated, shall also order the employer to pay the employee back pay, gratuities, compensatory damages and liquidated damages, and, in cases of repeated or willful violations, assess civil penalties.[132]

EMPLOYER RECORDS

Employers, under state and federal law, must maintain comprehensive records including hours worked, rate of pay, amount of overtime worked, deductions or additions to wages, and employee names, addresses, occupations, sex and social security numbers.[133] When wages are paid, Minnesota requires the employer to give the employee an earnings statement which includes:

- The name of the employee;

- The hourly rate of pay (if applicable);

- The total number of hours worked by the employee (unless exempt);

- The total amount of gross pay earned by the employee during that period;

- A list of deductions made from the employee's pay;

- The net amount of pay after all deductions are made;

- The date on which the pay period ends; and

- The legal name of the employer and the operating name of the employer if different from the legal name.[134]

EMPLOYEE BENEFIT PLANS:
ERISA, AND THE INTERNAL REVENUE CODE
IMPACT ON THE EMPLOYEE RELATIONSHIP

Each employer that offers any type of employee benefit to its employees should be familiar with its fundamental duties in establishing, administering, amending and terminating those pension and welfare benefit plans that are subject to the requirements of the Internal Revenue Code ("Code") and the Employee Retirement Income Security Act of 1974 ("ERISA"). Each time an employee is hired, takes a leave of absence, changes positions within the company, becomes disabled, or terminates employment, the employee's rights under the employer's benefit plans are usually affected, and require certain actions by the employer and/or the benefit plan administrator that must comply with the Code and ERISA.

There are two basic types of benefit plans governed by the Code and ERISA: 1) pension plans, which cover any retirement benefit or income deferral that is paid following termination of employment;[135] and 2) welfare benefit plans consisting of medical, dental, vision, life insurance, short term and long term disability insurance, severance, and medical reimbursements under cafeteria plans.[136] The Code contains requirements for favorable tax treatment of pension[137] and welfare[138] benefit plans and also establishes excise taxes for violations.[139] ERISA, on the other hand, establishes rules governing the administration[140] and fiduciary responsibility of plan sponsors, administrators and trustees[141] and provides procedures for participants who challenge the actions of the sponsor or administrator.[142] The Code and ERISA requirements are more complex and detailed for pension plans than for welfare plans. There are similar, but not always identical, requirements in the Code and ERISA governing the same conduct or minimum standards. However, a full discussion of these requirements is beyond the scope of this Guide.

As the sponsor of an employee benefit plan, the employer often will wear two hats: as the employer, it may act to amend a plan, terminate a plan, set contribution limits, and appoint and oversee third parties, such as the record keeper and trustees, who manage the plan and plan assets. Often times, however, the employer also assumes, by law or the terms of the plan, certain fiduciary duties in the administration of the plan and investment of plan assets. When the employer is acting in its role as employer, most of its acts are subject to the general business judgment rule that governs all other corporate actions. When the employer acts as a fiduciary, it must meet a higher standard: a fiduciary must act for the exclusive benefit of plan participants and beneficiaries, in compliance with employee benefit laws and the terms of the plan document, and must exercise the same degree of care and diligence that the person would use in their own personal affairs.[143] Persons who act in a fiduciary capacity may be personally liable for their actions, although an employer may indemnify employees and directors acting within the scope of their employment as a fiduciary for an employee benefit plan.[144] Persons handling plan assets must also be bonded against theft or embezzlement.[145]

As mentioned above, each time there is a significant change in the relationship between an employer and an employee, there usually is a related effect on the company's employee benefit plans. The following is a general, but by no means exhaustive, list of activities related to employee benefit plans that the employer or plan administrator should consider undertaking in those situations:

Newly Hired Employees (Or Employees Moving From Non-Eligible Into Eligible Employment):

- Provide employee with information regarding eligibility for an automatic enrollment in pension and welfare benefit plans and any conditions that apply, such as contributions toward premiums for certain coverages;
- Provide enrollment forms (if required) for the employee to complete and any other eligible persons (spouse and dependents), including authorization for payroll deductions, beneficiary designations and investment choices, if permitted;
- Determine if employee had creditable coverage under a prior health plan to avoid the application of any pre-existing conditions, exclusions, or limitations under the health plan;
- Provide initial COBRA notice to employee and to spouse or other dependents, if any, which details qualifying events permitting continuation of group health plan coverage by employee and any qualified beneficiaries;[146]
- Provide summary plan description or certificate of coverage summarizing material terms of each employee benefit plan within 90 days of the employee becoming covered under that plan;[147]
- Notify plan recordkeepers, administrators and payroll in order to initiate and/or complete the enrollment process and payroll withholding.

Begin Leave Of Absence (including Family & Medical Leave (FMLA) and qualified military leave):

- Determine which benefits will automatically continue, which benefits the employee may elect to continue, and which benefits, if any, terminate during the leave of absence;
- Determine if the leave triggers a change in family status that would permit a change in the employee's cafeteria plan election;
- Determine the effect on any participant loans from a pension plan and the rights the employee may have to a distribution or withdrawal of funds (employer must suspend loan repayment during period of qualified military leave);
- Determine whether the leave results in a qualifying event which will trigger COBRA or state law health plan continuation coverage rights;
- Determine whether the continuation of benefits will require contributions from the employee and determine whether such contributions are to be paid through any remaining payroll deductions or directly by the employee;

NOTE: For FMLA leave of absence, an employer is required to continue the employee's group health coverage during the period of FMLA leave as if the employee had continued to work, although the employee must continue to pay his or her share of the group health plan premiums in order to retain coverage during the leave. An employee on an FMLA leave of absence will not experience a COBRA qualifying event as a result of being on leave until he or she fails to return from FMLA leave or, if expressed earlier, makes it unequivocally clear to the employer that he or she does not intend on returning to employment.

- For highly compensated executives, determine if the leave triggers a separation from service that would require distribution under an on-qualified deferred compensation arrangement.
- Determine when benefits end if employee fails to return from leave.

Return To Employment After Leave Of Absence:

- Restart the employee payroll deductions for current contributions toward premiums and salary deferrals;
- For qualified military leave, determine whether employee is entitled to make up missed salary deferrals to pension plans for period of military leave and re-amortize any participant loan; also, credit any missed pension or profit sharing contributions;
- Determine whether the period of leave affects (counts) toward vesting, if any, or for benefit accruals under pension plans;
- Determine if the employee is permitted to repay any prior pension plan distribution received as a result of the leave.

Promotion, Increase In Compensation Or Change In Job Location:

- Determine whether any benefits for the employee change or if benefit levels increase;
- Check plan definition of "compensation" to determine if new or additional compensation items are included or excluded in determining pension or profit-sharing contributions, life and disability insurance levels, and if salary deferral election covers those new or additional items;
- If group health plan coverage is lost due to job relocation or change to non-covered employment, determine if COBRA or state law continuation coverage rights are triggered.

Termination Of Employment (Including Disability, Retirement, And Death While Employed):

- Provide COBRA or state law continuation notice to employee and qualified beneficiaries and determine whether any employer paid group health plan continuation coverage runs concurrent with, before or in place of, COBRA coverage;
- Determine if the employer owes any severance to the employee (e.g., Severance Pay Plan or terms of employment agreement);
- Notify recordkeepers, other plan administrators and insurers of change in the employee's employment status;
- Determine whether the employee is entitled to a year-end matching or profit-sharing contribution;
- Determine proper vesting for pension benefit payout;
- Determine the status of any outstanding qualified participant plan loan balance and the right to continue payment or acceleration of remaining debt;
- Process distributions from qualified plans, if a distribution is elected by participant;
- Determine the right to continued participation in the cafeteria plan for medical expense reimbursement and/or dependent day care reimbursement.

Miscellaneous Events:

The following events may also require action by the employer in connection with one or more employee benefit plans:

- Change in the terms of a benefit plan, which may trigger an obligation of the employer to provide employees a written supplement to the summary plan description, describing the plan changes (certain changes to health benefit plans must be communicated within 60 days of the change);[148]
- Plan year-end, which generally triggers an employer obligation to provide an annual statement of each participant's account in the qualified plan and provide annual notices as applicable about default deferral levels, default investments and fees associated with pension investment options[149] and to file with the IRS an annual tax return for pension and certain welfare plans;[150]
- A participant appeal of a denied claim for benefits, wherein the employer must comply with strict time periods and notice requirements under ERISA;[151]
- A participant's change in family status, such as divorce, birth or adoption, reaching age of majority, which may result in:
  - a loss of dependent status and separate COBRA continuation rights;
  - a court issuing a qualified domestic relations order (QDRO) dividing pension and profit sharing plan assets; or
  - a court issuing a qualified medical child support order (QMCSO) to require an employer's health plan cover an employee's children.
- Acquisition or sale of a business or assets, which may result in:
  - a reduction in force that may trigger an employer's obligation to provide affected employees with severance, a COBRA notice, and pension distribution or the buyer to acquire to hire additional employees;
  - transition of affected employees from seller's to buyer's benefit plans; or
  - the acquiring employer possibly assuming certain assets and liabilities of the seller's benefit plans.

Finally, a word of caution: employers who sponsor welfare and pension plans have faced increasing liability for errors in the administration of such plans, breach of fiduciary duty and conflicts of interest. Individual participants may sue pension plans directly for errors and certain losses caused by fiduciaries and service providers.[152] Often, a service provider to whom administration has been outsourced does not assume fiduciary status or requires in its service contract that the employer indemnify the service provider for any damages that result from the service provider's actions. Federal and state regulatory agencies have begun to scrutinize fee arrangements and conflicts of interest among service providers, which may in turn necessitate that the employer review provider service agreements and/or fee arrangements. Employers should carefully review plan documents and service provider contracts to determine the extent of any contractual indemnification, what relationship the service provider has to the plan and what fiduciary duties, if any, the employer and the service provider have undertaken under ERISA as applied to the benefit plan in question.

CONTINUATION OF GROUP HEALTH
AND LIFE INSURANCE COVERAGE

Most group health plans and group life insurance arrangements are subject to laws requiring that continuation of coverage be offered to employees, their spouses, and their dependents if certain events occur that would otherwise cause these persons to lose their coverage under the plan (for example, the termination of a covered employee's employment). These requirements are established by the federal Consolidated Omnibus Budget Reconciliation Act of 1985 ("COBRA")[153] and similar state laws.[154] Employers who offer these benefits must be aware of the applicable rules governing continuation of coverage, and must be prepared to provide the appropriate notices and election forms to covered individuals when these events occur.

The legal requirements in this area can be complex, and will depend on the type of plan the employer offers. For this reason, and because of the potential for liability in the event that an employer fails to comply with the continuation coverage requirements that apply to its plans, the employer should consult legal counsel regarding these requirements.

However, below is a brief overview of federal COBRA and Minnesota law with respect to an employer's continuation coverage requirements.

COBRA REQUIREMENTS

Employers and Plans Subject to COBRA

Employers (including corporations, partnerships, tax-exempt organizations and state and local governments) who sponsor group health plans and regularly employ 20 or more full and part-time employees are required to comply with federal COBRA law.[155] Certain small employer plans, certain church plans, and federal government plans are not subject to COBRA.[156]

A group health plan subject to COBRA must be maintained by an employer and provide medical care. "Medical care" includes medical, dental, vision and drug treatments, as well as coverage.[157]

Group health plans subject to COBRA include medical insurance arrangements maintained by employers, HMOs, self-insured medical reimbursement plans, employee assistance plans and health flexible spending arrangements, among others.[158]

Life insurance plans are not subject to federal COBRA.

COBRA Triggering Events

There are seven different "qualifying events" that trigger COBRA, which are:

(1) termination of a covered employee's employment (other than for gross misconduct);
(2) a reduction of a covered employee's hours of work;
(3) the covered employee's death;
(4) a divorce or legal separation from the covered employee;
(5) a dependent child of the covered employee ceases to be a dependent under the terms of the plan;

(6) the covered employee becomes entitled to Medicare; and

(7) an employer bankruptcy (retiree plans only).[159]

Employers generally only have an obligation to offer COBRA continuation coverage when an individual covered under the plan experiences a qualifying event. In order for a qualifying event to occur, there must be both a triggering qualifying event (listed above) and a resulting loss in plan coverage.[160] For example, an employer's termination of its health plan will not require the employer to offer COBRA coverage, because, while there is a loss of plan coverage, no triggering event occurred that resulted in the loss of coverage.

Special Rules

Special COBRA rules apply to leaves of absence, particularly leaves under the Family and Medical Leave Act. Under IRS COBRA regulations, a COBRA qualifying event does not occur when an employee takes a leave under the FMLA. Rather, a qualifying event occurs when:

- an employee (or dependent child or spouse of the employee) is covered on the day before the first day of FMLA leave under the employer's group health plan;

- the employee does not return to employment with the employer at the end of the leave; and,

- the employee (or dependent child or spouse of the employee) would, in the absence of COBRA coverage, lose coverage under the group health plan prior to the end of the maximum coverage period.[161]

Essentially, an employee will experience a COBRA qualifying event when he or she fails to return from FMLA leave, or, if earlier, when he or she unequivocally informs the employer that he or she does not intend on returning to employment.[162] The COBRA maximum coverage period is measured without regard to any state-required continuation coverage.[163]

An employer should consult with legal counsel for further advice in this area, as well as in other specialized instances, such as in the context of mergers and acquisitions.

Also, if an employer is offering a departing employee severance pay pursuant to a severance agreement, the severance agreement should specifically address COBRA and how the employer will handle it. Employers may agree to pay a departing employee's COBRA premium for a short period (e.g., 3 months) of the COBRA coverage, so long as the employee elects such coverage. The employer's failure to properly deal with COBRA in a severance agreement could create unintended liabilities for the employer and the plan.

Offering COBRA

Generally speaking, an employer needs to offer COBRA continuation coverage to every person (known as a "qualified beneficiary") who will lose group health coverage under the plan as a result of a qualifying event.[164] Each qualified beneficiary under the plan has an independent right to elect COBRA.[165] The employer must offer COBRA continuation coverage that is identical to the coverage the plan provided for similarly situated qualified beneficiaries prior to the qualifying event.

Basic Maximum COBRA Coverage Periods

The maximum length of COBRA coverage the employer will offer depends upon the qualifying event. For termination of employment or reduction in hours, 18 months is the maximum coverage period (24 months for active military personnel). For death of the employee, divorce or legal separation, a child's loss of dependent status under the plan, or an employee's entitlement to Medicare, the maximum coverage period is 36 months.[166] Typically, COBRA coverage will begin on the date of the triggering event. In certain cases, the 18-month maximum coverage period can be extended through multiple qualifying events or a qualified beneficiary's disability, for example.[167]

Termination of COBRA Coverage Prior to Expiration of Maximum COBRA Coverage Period

A plan is permitted (but not required) to terminate a qualified beneficiary's COBRA coverage prior to the end of the maximum coverage period in the following situations:

- the qualified beneficiary does not pay the required premium on time;
- the qualified beneficiary becomes covered under another group health plan after electing COBRA coverage;
- the qualified beneficiary becomes entitled to Medicare after electing COBRA;
- under the disability extension, a qualified beneficiary who was disabled is determined by the Social Security Administration to no longer be disabled;
- the employer ceases to provide or maintain any group health plan for any of its employees; or
- for cause (such as for filing a fraudulent benefit claim).[168]

COBRA Notice Requirements

COBRA requires employers and/or plan administrators to provide plan participants with various notices and other written communication at certain times.

Under COBRA, a group health plan must provide an Initial or "General" COBRA Notice to covered employees and their covered spouses at the time of commencement of coverage under the plan.[169] In 2004, the federal Department of Labor (DOL) finalized COBRA regulations that make significant changes to COBRA notice obligations applying to plan years beginning on or after November 26, 2004.[170]

1. Initial COBRA Notice

The Plan Administrator has the obligation to send the Initial COBRA Notice to the covered employee (and his or her spouse, if any) when the employee (and spouse, if any) becomes covered under the group health plan. The Initial Notice (sometimes referred to as the "General Notice") contains general information about participants' COBRA rights and obligations.[171] Under the 2004 DOL final regulations, the Plan Administrator must deliver the Initial Notice to the participant within 90 days after coverage begins. The final regulations require that the Initial Notice contain the following items:

- the plan name and address and the name, address, and telephone number of a party from whom additional information about the plan and continuation coverage can be obtained;
- a general description of COBRA continuation coverage;
- a description of qualified beneficiaries' obligations to provide a qualifying event notice to the plan administrator and related procedures (for example, notification of a divorce or child reaching maximum age for coverage);
- a description of qualified beneficiaries' disability notice requirements and related procedures;
- an explanation of the importance of participants/qualified beneficiaries to keep the plan administrator informed of their current address; and
- a statement that more complete information regarding COBRA continuation coverage rights is available from the plan administrator and from the plan SPD.[172]

A sample form of the Initial (or General) Notice is available at www.dol.gov/ebsa/ modelgeneralnotice.doc. Employers and Plan Administrators are cautioned that this Notice will require tailoring to the particular group health plan. Thus, the employer or Plan Administrator should consult with legal counsel for revisions prior to use.

2. <u>COBRA Election Notice</u>

The Plan Administrator also has the obligation to send a COBRA Election Notice to each qualified beneficiary who will lose plan coverage as a result of a qualifying event. The Election Notice contains information about a qualified beneficiary's continuation coverage rights and obligations with respect to a qualifying event, and is typically accompanied by a COBRA Election Form.[173]

The Plan Administrator must send out the Election Notice within 14 days of the time it receives notice that a qualifying event has occurred. The DOL's final 2004 regulations list 14 required items that must appear in the Election Notice.[174] They are:

- plan name and address;
- identification of the qualifying event;
- identification of each qualified beneficiary and the date the plan coverage will terminate;
- a statement regarding each qualified beneficiary's independent right to elect COBRA continuation coverage;
- an explanation of how to elect COBRA continuation coverage;
- an explanation of the consequences of failing to elect COBRA continuation coverage;
- a description of the COBRA continuation coverage;
- an explanation of the duration of COBRA continuation coverage;
- a description of the circumstances under which COBRA coverage may be extended;
- a description of the plan's requirements concerning a qualified beneficiary's obligation to provide notice to the plan of a second qualifying event and notice of a Social Security disability determination, and related procedures;
- a description of the COBRA premium amount;
- a description of the plan's COBRA premium payment procedures;
- an explanation of the importance of qualified beneficiaries to keep the plan informed of current address; and

- a statement that more complete information regarding COBRA continuation coverage rights is available from the Plan Administrator and from the plan SPD.

A sample form of the Election Notice is available at www.dol.gov/ebsa/modelelectionnotice.doc. Employers and Plan Administrators are cautioned that this Notice will require tailoring to the particular group health plan and, therefore, they should consult with legal counsel for revisions prior to use.

3. Notice Of Termination Of COBRA Coverage

The DOL's 2004 final regulations require that a plan administrator that terminates COBRA coverage prior to the end of the maximum continuation coverage period provide each affected qualified beneficiary with a notice that specifies when his or her COBRA coverage will be terminated.[175] Plan administrators can provide the Notice of Termination of COBRA Coverage along with the required HIPAA certificate, which must also be provided to a qualified beneficiary when coverage ends.

4. Notice Of Unavailability Of COBRA Coverage

The DOL's 2004 final regulations also require that the plan administrator provide a qualified beneficiary with a Notice of Unavailability of COBRA Coverage when it determines that such qualified beneficiary is not entitled to COBRA coverage (or to an extension of the maximum COBRA period) after receiving notice from the individual of a qualifying event, a notice of a second qualifying event, or notice of a disability.[176]

5. Qualifying Event Notice

In order for a plan administrator to issue an Election Notice to a qualified beneficiary, it has to first receive notice of when a qualifying event occurs. In general, employers are obligated to inform the plan administrator of certain qualifying events within 30 days of their occurrence, which include:

- death of a covered employee;
- termination (other than for gross misconduct) or reduction in hours of the covered employee;
- the covered employee becomes entitled to Medicare; or employer bankruptcy.[177]

Under the DOL's 2004 final regulations, covered employees and qualified beneficiaries also have a duty to inform the plan administrator of certain qualifying events,[178] generally within 60 days of their occurrence.

The notices required from covered employees and qualifying beneficiaries include:

- notice of a qualifying event that is a divorce or legal separation of a covered employee from his or her spouse, and/or a dependent child's losing dependent status under the plan;
- notice of second qualifying events, including the death of a covered employee, divorce or legal separation from the covered employee, the covered employee becoming entitled to Medicare benefits, and a dependent child ceasing to be a dependent under the terms of the plan;

- notice of a disability determination from the Social Security Administration; and
- notice of a change in disability status according to the Social Security Administration.

Under the DOL's final 2004 regulations, plans must establish reasonable procedures for employees and qualified beneficiaries to provide notice to the plan administrator, and describe these procedures in the plan's SPD.[179]

COBRA Elections

COBRA continuation coverage is not automatically extended to a qualified beneficiary; he or she must affirmatively elect such coverage.

Under COBRA, a qualified beneficiary has 60 days after the date that plan coverage terminates, or if later, 60 days after the date of the election notice to the qualified beneficiary from the plan administrator, to elect COBRA coverage.[180]

When the date of the election notice is later than the loss of coverage date, the general rule is that the 60-day notice period starts to run from the date the election notice is "sent," although at least one court case has held that the period does not begin to run until the qualified beneficiary actually receives the election notice.[181] Remember that each qualified beneficiary has a separate right to elect COBRA among the different types of coverage he or she had prior to the qualifying event.[182] The covered employee or spouse may elect the COBRA continuation coverage for other qualified beneficiaries, although a spouse may not decline coverage on behalf of the other spouse.[183]

COBRA Premiums and Payment

A plan may charge the qualified beneficiary for the cost of COBRA continuation coverage, but it is not required to do so.[184]

The maximum COBRA premium for one month of continuation coverage is 102% of the applicable premium.[185] The additional 2% represents an administrative fee that the plan administrator may charge. Under the disability extension, the plan may charge the disabled qualified beneficiary up to 150% of the applicable premium.[186] Employers should note, however, that the recently passed stimulus bill, the American Recovery and Reinvestment Act of 2009 (the "ARRA"), includes provisions to assist with the payment of COBRA premiums for certain terminated workers. Under the stimulus bill provisions, the federal government will subsidize 65% of the COBRA premiums for certain assistance-eligible individuals ("AEIs") for a period of time. The provisions of the ARRA also provide certain recently unemployed people the ability to re-enroll into the COBRA plan, even if they had declined coverage in the past. Employers should consult with legal counsel regarding the COBRA provisions contained in the ARRA.

The COBRA premium may be different depending upon the type of coverage the qualified beneficiary elects. A plan may require that the qualified beneficiary pay the initial premium for COBRA continuation coverage as early as 45 days from the date of his or her COBRA election.[187] Thereafter, premiums are generally due on the first day of the month, subject to a 30-day (or longer) grace period.[188]

Plans are not required to send out monthly bills, although some do. A plan may terminate a qualified beneficiary's COBRA coverage for his or her nonpayment of premiums after the expiration of any applicable grace periods. In that case, the plan administrator must send the qualified beneficiary the Notice of Termination of Coverage because the plan is terminating coverage prior to the expiration of the maximum coverage period.

Penalties for Failure to Comply with COBRA

- The IRS may assess excise tax penalties of $100 per day (up to $200 per day if more than one qualified beneficiary is affected from the same family) for each day a plan fails to comply with COBRA.[189]
- For single employer plans, the overall limit on the liability for tax penalties for failures due to reasonable cause (and not willful neglect) is $500,000.[190]
- Qualified beneficiaries may sue to recover statutory penalties of $110 per day for a plan's failure to provide him or her with an Initial COBRA or Election Notice under COBRA.[191]
- Qualified beneficiaries can sue to recover COBRA coverage allegedly due under the plan. In these cases, the Plan Sponsor, Plan Administrator or the insurance company can become obligated to provide COBRA coverage.
- Other relief may be available to qualified beneficiaries based on a plan's failure to provide him or her with an initial or election notice.[192]
- The Court is permitted in a COBRA lawsuit to award attorneys' fees and interest to the prevailing party.[193]

MINNESOTA STATE LAW REQUIREMENTS

Group Health Plan Continuation Coverage and Conversion Requirements

Continuation Coverage

Minnesota law requires that insured group health plans and plans established by employers through HMOs allow covered employees who are voluntarily or involuntarily terminated from employment to elect to continue coverage for herself and her dependents.[194] Termination does not include discharge for gross misconduct.[195] The employee is eligible to continue coverage for 18 months after termination, or until he or she becomes covered under another group health plan, whichever is shorter.[196]

The employer has the duty to inform the employee within 10 days after his or her termination or layoff of:

- the right to elect to continue coverage;
- the amount the employee must pay monthly to the employer to retain coverage;
- the manner in which and where the payment to the employer must be made; and
- the time by which the employee must make payments to the employer in order to retain coverage.[197]

The notice must be in writing and sent by first class mail. The employee has 60 days within which to elect coverage.

<u>Conversion to Individual Policy</u>

Group health plans required to follow Minnesota law with regard to continuation coverage (above) are also required to allow a covered employee, surviving spouse, or other dependent to obtain from the insurer the option to obtain an individual policy of insurance at the end of the continuation coverage period. The employee, spouse, or dependent does not have to provide further evidence of insurability to obtain the conversion policy and coverage must not be interrupted.[198]

Group Life Insurance Plan Continuation Coverage and Conversion Requirements

<u>Continuation Coverage</u>

Minnesota law requires group life insurance plans to permit employees who are voluntarily or involuntarily terminated from employment the option to elect to continue the coverage for the employee and his or her dependents. Termination does not include discharge for gross misconduct.[199]

The employee is eligible to continue coverage for 18 months after termination, or until the employee becomes covered under another group life insurance plan, whichever is shorter.[200]

The employer has the duty to inform the employee upon termination or layoff from employment of:

- the employee's right to continue the coverage;
- the amount the employee must pay monthly to the employer to retain the coverage;
- the manner in which and where the employee must send the payment; and
- the time by which the employee must make payments to the employer in order to retain coverage.

The employee has 60 days within which to elect coverage. Notice must be in writing and sent by first class mail.[201]

<u>Conversion to Individual Policy</u>

Group life insurance plans required to follow Minnesota law with regard to continuation coverage (above) are also required to allow a covered employee, a surviving spouse, or dependent the ability to obtain from the insurer an individual policy of insurance providing the same or substantially the same benefits. The employee, spouse, or dependent does not have to provide further evidence of insurability to obtain the conversion policy and coverage must not be interrupted.[202]

HIPAA PORTABILITY AND PRIVACY

Employer group health plans are also subject to the Health Insurance Portability and Accountability Act of 1996 ("HIPAA").[203]

HIPAA Portability Requirements

HIPAA's portability, special enrollment, pre-existing condition exclusions restrictions, and nondiscrimination requirements apply generally to group health plans. HIPAA prohibits group health plans from discriminating against employees based on their health status and grants certain health plan enrollment rights to employees. The main purpose of HIPAA, however, is to ensure that workers who change jobs will not lose health insurance coverage due to exclusions for pre-existing conditions.

Under HIPAA, group health plans may not exclude coverage for pre-existing conditions for longer than 12 months (18 months for late enrollees).[204] In addition, any exclusion period is reduced by an employee's period of coverage under a prior employer's group health plan. The pre-existing exclusion period runs from the enrollment date, or if there is a waiting period, from the first day of the waiting period.[205]

Group health plans must provide "certificates of creditable coverage" to employees who lose coverage, and accept such certificates from other plans.[206] Insurance companies will often take responsibility for complying with HIPAA's notice and administrative requirements, but employers with insured plans should verify that their insurer is complying with HIPAA. Employers that maintain self-funded health plans are on their own, and should seek assistance from legal counsel to develop the appropriate notices and forms (or contract with a third party administrator for HIPAA compliance services).

The final HIPAA portability regulations contain a new model certificate of creditable coverage containing a new required educational statement.[207] The final regulations apply to plan years beginning on or after July 1, 2005. The model certificate for group health plans can be found at http://www.dol.gov/ebsa/hipaamodelnotice.doc. Employers and Plan Administrators are cautioned that this Notice will require tailoring to the particular group health plan, and therefore, they should consult with legal counsel for revisions prior to use.

HIPAA Privacy Standards

When HIPAA was originally enacted, it did not contain detailed privacy standards, but required further regulations to be promulgated. The HIPAA final privacy regulations were published on August 14, 2002, and impose rules surrounding the use and disclosure of individuals' protected health information. The recently passed stimulus bill, the American Recovery and Reinvestment Act of 2009 ("ARRA"), includes provisions that will significantly change the HIPAA privacy regulations for both "covered entities" and "business associates" (defined below). Consult with legal counsel to determine the extent to which the HIPAA privacy regulations apply and the steps required to comply.

Covered Entities

HIPAA's privacy standards only apply to "covered entities." Group health plans, health care providers, and health care clearinghouses are considered "covered entities" required to comply with the HIPAA privacy rules.[208] While employers are technically not covered under the privacy rules, they will essentially have to comply if they sponsor a group health plan and perform administrative functions which involve handling protected health information on behalf of the plan.

Group health plans with fewer than 50 participants and that are administered by the employer are specifically excluded from the definition of a group health plan, and are therefore not subject to HIPAA's privacy standards.[209]

Deadlines to Comply

Covered entities were required to comply with the privacy rules by April 14, 2003. Small health plans (those with annual gross receipts of less than $5 million in claims or premiums) had until April 14, 2004 to comply.

Protected Health Information

Protected Health Information, otherwise known as "PHI," is defined under HIPAA's privacy regulations to be individually identifiable information that is maintained or transmitted by a covered entity, and is subject to the following specific exclusions:

- individually identifiable health information contained in education records covered by the Family Educational Rights and Privacy Act (FERPA):

- health care records of students in post-secondary degree programs; and

- employment records held by a covered entity in its role as an employer.[210]

Use and Disclosure

Covered entities are only permitted to use or disclose PHI as set forth under the privacy standards. Under these rules, covered entities may use or disclose PHI for treatment, payment or health care operations purposes, which are specifically defined.[211] A signed authorization is usually required for further use or disclosure,[212] although there are exceptions, such as to avoid a serious threat to health or safety, for public policy purposes, for public health activities, or as required by law, among others.[213]

Individual Rights

HIPAA's privacy rules guarantee individuals specific rights with respect to their health information, including the right to:

- receive a copy of the covered entity's Notice of Privacy Practices;
- inspect and copy protected health information contained in their designated record set;
- receive an accounting of disclosures made by the covered entity;
- amend or correct inaccurate or incomplete PHI; and
- request additional restrictions on the use and disclosure of their own PHI.[214]

Privacy Notice

Covered entities are required to develop and provide a copy of their privacy practices to each individual that is the subject of the PHI. The regulations specify specific information that the notice must contain, including the types of uses and disclosures that the covered entity is permitted to make.[215] A fully insured group health plan's insurer will generally have the obligation to provide the notice to the insured. Self-funded plans must provide their own notice.

Administrative Safeguards

HIPAA's privacy standards require covered entities to take specific actions designed to protect the privacy of an individual's PHI, including, but not limited to:

- designating a privacy official who is responsible for developing and implementing privacy policies and procedures;
- designating a contact person responsible for receiving complaints;
- providing training to all members of the covered entity's workforce on policies and procedures with respect to PHI;
- establishing safeguards to protect the privacy of the PHI (physical and technical);
- developing a complaint procedure;
- developing appropriate sanction/disciplinary procedures for employees who violate the privacy rules; and
- implementing policies and procedures to comply with the privacy rules.[216]

Business Associates

Business associates are outside entities or individuals that assist covered entities in performing their functions. HIPAA's privacy rule requires that a covered entity enter into a written contract or other arrangement with the business associate in order to disclose PHI to the business associate, and in order to allow the business associate to create or receive PHI on behalf of the covered entity.[217] For example, business associates can be providers of legal, actuarial, accounting, consulting, management or financial services.[218]

Fully Insured Group Health Plans

Employers who sponsor fully insured group health plans and do not create, maintain or receive PHI (i.e., are "hands-off") will have vastly reduced obligations under HIPAA's privacy standards. In this situation, the requirements to comply with the use and disclosure rules, provide the HIPAA privacy notice, comply with the various individual rights, and comply with HIPAA's administrative safeguards are imposed upon the insurer.[219]

HIPAA's Privacy Standards Enforcement

Individuals do not have a private cause of action when their HIPAA privacy rights have been violated. However, such individuals may file a complaint with the federal Health and Human Services' ("HHS") Office of Civil Rights, which will accept and investigate complaints. The HHS has the authority to impose civil penalties of up to $100 per violation (maximum of $25,000 per calendar year) for violation of HIPAA's privacy rules against the offending covered entity.[220] In addition, criminal penalties may apply if a person knowingly misuses a unique health identifier or improperly discloses or obtains individually identifiable health information.[221] The criminal penalties can be fines of up to $50,000 or imprisonment for up to a year, or both, for knowing violations, or fines of up to $250,000 or imprisonment for up to ten years, or both, where the offense is with the intent to sell, transfer or use the individually identifiable health information for commercial advantage, personal gain or malicious harm.

The U.S. Department of Justice has the authority to enforce HIPAA's criminal penalties.

For More Information

The U.S. Department of Health and Human Services' website is located at www.hhs.gov and provides answers to frequently asked questions regarding HIPAA privacy compliance.

However, because HIPAA's privacy standards are so complex and detailed, plan sponsors should consult with legal counsel to ensure proper and complete HIPAA compliance.

WORKPLACE ISSUES

DISCRIMINATION IN GENERAL

The Minnesota Human Rights Act provides that it is an unfair employment practice for any employer to:

- Refuse to hire, or maintain a system of employment which unreasonably excludes a person seeking employment;

- Discharge an employee; or

- Discriminate against a person with respect to hiring, tenure, compensation, terms, upgrading, conditions, facilities or privileges of employment

based upon any of the following: race, color, creed, religion, national origin, sex, marital status, status with regard to public assistance, membership or activity in a local commission, disability, sexual orientation or age.[222] When discrimination is referred to anywhere in this Guide, the reference is to any adverse employment action (e.g. termination, demotion, etc.) against a member of any group (i.e. "protected class") protected by local, state, or federal law.

Title VII of the Civil Rights Acts of 1964 and 1991 is the primary federal statute prohibiting discrimination in the workplace. Under Title VII, which applies to employers with 15 or more employees, the protected classes are: race, color, religion, sex and national origin. The Age Discrimination in Employment Act is a federal law that prohibits discrimination on the basis of age and applies to employers with 20 or more employees.[223] Disability is also a protected class under federal law for private employers with 15 or more employees under the Americans with Disabilities Act.[224] Employers should be aware that part-time employees and contingent workers may be counted as "employees" for purposes of coverage under federal law.[225]

It is beyond the scope of this Guide to describe all of the different ways in which employees can attempt to prove discrimination and how employers can best defend against such claims. However, as a general matter, discrimination claims often turn on the issue of whether the employer took some adverse employment action for a legitimate business reason or whether the employer's stated reason is a pretext for discrimination. The United States Supreme Court and Minnesota Supreme Court have ruled that disbelief of the employer's stated reason for an adverse employment action may infer that a discriminatory reason was the real reason for the action and that an employee need not produce additional evidence in order to prove discrimination.[226] Thus, it is very important in any adverse employment action for the employer to carefully consider the reasons for its actions and to communicate those reasons accurately and consistently to the affected employee. Incomplete or inconsistent explanations may leave an employer vulnerable to the allegation that it acted unlawfully.

PERMITTED EMPLOYMENT PRACTICES

The following employment practices, which could otherwise be construed as discriminatory, are legally permissible:[227]

- An employer may refuse to hire an individual for a reason which constitutes a "bona fide occupational qualification." For example, religion is a bona fide occupational qualification for certain positions in religious organizations.

- An employer may follow a bona fide seniority system which requires differences in wages, hiring priorities, layoff priorities, vacation credit, job assignments and the like, as long as these differences are based on seniority and are not a subterfuge to evade discrimination laws.

- Certain differences in benefits will not be considered evidence of age discrimination so long as those differences are based on cost and the cost of benefits for individuals of all ages is reasonably equivalent.

- Certain organizations whose primary function is to provide youth activities, as well as religious and fraternal associations, are exempt from discriminatory prohibitions related to sexual orientation. (See Sexual Orientation Discrimination discussed later in this Guide).

- Pre-employment physical examinations and pre-employment testing are permitted under certain circumstances (discussed under the Hiring Process section of this Guide).

- Obtaining medical information from an employee after employment has commenced is permissible, with the consent of the employee, for the following purposes:

  - To assess the employee's continuing ability to perform the job;

  - To determine employee health insurance eligibility;

  - To comply with mandates of local, state or federal law;

  - To assess the need to reasonably accommodate a disabled employee; or

  - To further or implement another legitimate business reason not otherwise prohibited by law.

All medical information obtained from an employee must be collected on separate forms and maintained in separate medical files as confidential medical records.

DISABILITY DISCRIMINATION

MINNESOTA LAW

Under the Minnesota Human Rights Act (which generally applies to employers with one or more employees), individuals with a disability are protected from discrimination in employment. A disabled person is one who has a physical, sensory or mental impairment that materially limits one or more major life activities, has a record of such impairment, or is regarded as having such an impairment.[228]

Qualified disabled persons (i.e., a disabled person who, with or without reasonable accommodation, can perform the essential functions required of all employees performing and/or all applicants for the job in question) are further protected under Minnesota law.[229] Specifically, employers with 15 or more employees are required to make a reasonable accommodation to the known disability of a qualified disabled person, unless the employer can demonstrate that the accommodation would impose an undue hardship upon the business or organization.[230] An individual who has a condition that results from alcohol or drug abuse and prevents that person from performing the essential functions of the job in question or poses a direct threat to property or safety of others is not a qualified disabled person.

"Reasonable accommodation" means the steps that the employer must take to accommodate the physical or mental limitations of a qualified disabled person that are actually known (or should have been known) to the employer. Reasonable accommodation may include, but does not necessarily require, the following:

- Making facilities readily accessible to and usable by disabled persons;

- Some job restructuring and reassignment to vacant positions which the disabled person is qualified to perform (but not creating new positions);

- Modified work schedules (which may include reduced hours, although an employer is not always required to offer part-time work as a reasonable accommodation);

- Acquisition or modification of equipment or devices; and

- Provision of aides on a temporary or periodic basis.

In determining whether an accommodation constitutes an undue hardship, the following factors should be considered:

- The overall size of the business, including number of employees and number and type of facilities;

- The type of operation, including the composition and structure of the work force and the number of employees at the location where the employment would occur;

- The nature and cost of the needed accommodation;

- The reasonable ability to finance the accommodation at each site; and

- Documented good faith efforts to explore less expensive alternatives, including consultation with the disabled person or with knowledgeable disabled persons or organizations.

In determining whether an employee can safely and adequately perform his or her job, in spite of a disability, and what accommodations may be necessary, the employer is advised to rely on the advice of a competent physician. The employer should provide the physician with an accurate job description and request suggestions as to accommodation if the employee is unable to work without some form of assistance.

Please see the sections in this Guide relating to workers' compensation and the Family and Medical Leave Act dealing with employer responsibilities toward individuals who have workplace-related injuries and are covered under Minnesota workers' compensation law and who are entitled to family and medical leave. Employers should realize that their duties to their disabled employees should be analyzed with disability discrimination, workers' compensation and family and medical leave laws in mind.

FEDERAL LAW

The Americans with Disabilities Act[231] ("ADA"), broadly prohibits discrimination on the basis of disability in employment (as well as in public services, public accommodations, public services operated by private entities, and telecommunications) and requires reasonable accommodation of a qualified individual with a disability. The ADA generally prohibits discrimination against a qualified individual with a disability, because of the individual's disability, in all aspects of employment, including both the application process and the terms and conditions of employment such as compensation, advancement, training and discharge. The ADA applies to employers with 15 or more employees. The term "employer" is collectively used to refer to private employers, state and local governments, employment agencies, labor unions, and joint labor management committees. The term also includes "agents" of the employer, e.g., foremen, supervisors, or even agencies used to conduct background checks of applicants.[232]

In order to be "disabled" under the ADA, a person must be substantially limited in one or more major life activities such as seeing, hearing, walking, talking, or performing other functions.

A "qualified individual with a disability" is a person who, with or without reasonable accommodation, can perform the essential functions of the job. The same principles under Minnesota law regarding reasonable accommodation apply under federal law. A written job description that is prepared prior to advertising or interviewing applicants should state the essential functions of the job. Such job descriptions can be considered evidence of those essential functions.

Employers may deny employment to an applicant or remove an employee from a particular position if a job presents a direct threat to the person's health even if there is no threat to others in the workplace.[233]

Employers ordinarily may enforce their seniority policies in assigning jobs, hours, and other conditions of employment notwithstanding requests by disabled employees for reasonable accommodation of their particular situation.[234] However, employees requesting changes in jobs, hours or other working conditions on account of a disability should be permitted to show special circumstances justifying a deviation from the seniority system, such as the employer's practice of unilaterally and frequently making changes to the seniority system.

On January 1, 2009 the ADA Amendments Act of 2008 ("ADAAA") became law. The ADAAA significantly broadens the coverage of the ADA so that more employees with less severe impairments will be protected by the definition of "disability."[235] This means that employers will need to reevaluate the handling of employee disability and accommodation issues.

The ADAAA amendments do not change the wording of the disability definition—the definition of "disability" remains: (1) a physical or mental impairment that substantially limits one or more major life activities; (2) a record of such impairment; or (3) being regarded as having such an impairment." Under prior law, however, Courts construed the term "disability" narrowly to create a "demanding standard" for qualifying as disabled under the ADA.[236] The ADAAA amendments drastically change this standard, and explicitly mandate that the definition of "disability" is now to be construed by the courts in favor of broad coverage of individuals.

Similarly, the ADAAA amendments require the phrase "substantially limits" to be interpreted expansively in favor of broad coverage of individuals. Under the ADAAA, an impairment that substantially limits one major life activity need not limit other major life activities in order to be a disability. In addition, an impairment that is episodic or in remission will be deemed a disability if it would substantially limit a major life activity when active.

The ADAAA amendments include a non-exhaustive list of "major life activities." These activities include: caring for oneself, performing manual tasks, seeing, hearing, eating, sleeping, walking, standing, lifting, bending, speaking, breathing, learning, reading, concentrating, thinking, communicating, and working. The amendments also include new language stating that the operation of "major bodily functions" is a major life activity. Major bodily functions include functions of the immune system, normal cell growth, digestive, bowel, bladder, neurological, brain, respiratory, circulatory, endocrine, and reproductive functions.

Prior law allowed employers to take into account corrective devices and mitigating measures (such as medications and medical equipment) when considering whether an employee was "disabled" for purposes of the ADA.[237] The ADAAA amendments directly override prior law with respect to mitigating measures and corrective devices. Now, the ADAAA amendments mandate that the determination of whether an impairment substantially limits a major life activity must be made *without regard to the effects of mitigating measures*. The language of the ADAAA contains an exception for the effect of ordinary eyeglasses and contact lenses, which may still be taken into account.

As noted above, the ADA protects individuals who are disabled as well as those individuals who employers wrongly regard as being disabled. The ADAAA amendments provide that an employee is "regarded as" disabled if the employee was subjected to discrimination because of an actual or perceived impairment, without more. It does not matter whether the impairment actually limits or is perceived to limit a major life activity. Transitory and minor impairments, however, cannot be the basis of a "regarded as" claim. Transitory impairments are impairments with an actual or expected duration of six months or less.

Employers are strongly encouraged to consult with legal counsel regarding disability assessments and reasonable accommodation issues, particularly in light of the ADAAA amendments.

SPECIFIC ACTS OF DISCRIMINATION

The ADA prohibits:

- Limiting, segregating or classifying a job applicant or employee in a way that adversely affects his or her opportunities or status because of a disability;

- Participating in a contractual relationship, e.g., with an employment agency or labor union, that has the effect of discriminating against a disabled applicant or employee;

- Utilizing standards, criteria or methods of administration that have the effect of discrimination on the basis of disability or that perpetuate discrimination;

- Excluding or otherwise denying equal jobs or benefits to a qualified individual because of the known disability of an individual with whom the qualified individual is known to associate;

- Not making reasonable accommodation to the known physical or mental limitations of an applicant or employee with a disability unless the employer can demonstrate that the accommodation would impose an undue hardship on business operations;

- Denying employment opportunities to a qualified applicant or employee with a disability, if the denial is based on the employer's need to make reasonable accommodation to the individual's physical or mental impairment;

- Using qualification standards, employment tests or other selection criteria that screen out or tend to screen out individuals with disabilities unless the standards, tests or other selection criteria are shown to be job related and consistent with business necessity;

- Failing to select and administer employment tests in a manner that will effectively ensure that test results reflect the skills, aptitude or other factors that are being measured, and not the impairment;

- Harassing a disabled person by creating a hostile or offensive working environment on account of the person's disability; and

- Retaliating against any individual who opposes a practice prohibited by the ADA or enjoys rights under the ADA.

An employee or applicant who is engaged in the illegal use of drugs is not protected by the ADA. The employer may not, however, discriminate against a qualified individual who has successfully completed or is participating in a supervised drug rehabilitation program and is no longer engaged in the illegal use of drugs. An employer may adopt or administer reasonable policies and procedures, including drug testing, to ensure that the individual is no longer engaged in the illegal use of drugs. If the employer intends to use drug testing for this purpose, the employer should consult legal counsel in order to ensure that its drug testing policy (discussed in the Alcohol and Drug Problems in the Workplace section of this Guide) complies with Minnesota law. The ADA expressly allows an employer to:

- Prohibit the illegal use of drugs and the use of alcohol at the workplace;

- Require that employees not be under the influence of alcohol or not be engaged in the illegal use of drugs in the workplace;

- Require conformity with the federal Drug Free Workplace Act; and

- Hold an employee who engages in the illegal use of drugs or who is an alcoholic to the same qualification standards for employment or job performance and behavior to which the employer holds other employees, even if unsatisfactory performance or behavior is related to drug use or alcoholism by the employee.

In addition to individuals currently engaged in the use of illegal drugs, the following individuals are not protected by the Act: transvestites, homosexuals, bisexuals, transsexuals, pedophiles, exhibitionists, voyeurs, individuals with gender identity disorders not resulting from physical impairments or other sexual disorders, compulsive gamblers, kleptomaniacs, pyromaniacs or persons with psychoactive substance use disorders resulting from current illegal use of drugs.

The ADA's provisions are to be coordinated with the provisions of the federal Rehabilitation Act of 1973, which currently protects employees and applicants of employers who qualify as government contractors. The ADA is enforced by the Equal Employment Opportunity Commission (the "EEOC") which has issued extensive regulations interpreting the provisions of the ADA.[238] The EEOC also periodically issues written statements called Guidances that identify the EEOC's interpretation of various provisions of the ADA. For example, the EEOC has issued Guidances on the meaning of "mental impairment," disability related inquiries and medical examinations of employees and job applicants, reasonable accommodation and undue hardship, and related ADA issues. Employers should note that such regulations or Guidances may be modified or revised in light of the ADAAA amendments. Required posters describing employees' and applicants' rights under the ADA are available from the EEOC's Minnesota Office at (612) 335-4040 or (800) 669-4000.

AIDS

An individual who has AIDS (or another infectious disease) is protected as a qualified disabled person under Minnesota law and the ADA so long as that person is able to perform the essential functions of the job and is not a health or safety threat to his or her coworkers. Courts have cast doubt on an employer's ability to legally prove that someone with HIV (and possibly AIDS) actually poses a risk to the health or safety of others.[239]

However, while the risk of AIDS infection may be remote in most cases, an employer who knows that one of its employees has AIDS has a responsibility to its other employees to seek expert advice as to the risks of infection and preventive steps which may be necessary. AIDS-related information, as with all medical information relating to employees, must be kept in separate medical files, and treated as confidential medical records.

PREGNANCY

Pregnancy is excluded as a disability under the ADA, but pregnancy-related conditions may constitute protected disabilities. Pregnancy is also a circumstance which may give rise to a claim of sex discrimination. A pregnant employee who is unable to work due to pregnancy or childbirth is entitled to the same disability plan benefits which are available for non-pregnancy related disorders. In addition, the benefits and conditions of employment extended to employees with other physical and mental disorders must be extended to pregnant employees. For example, if a male employee has a heart attack and is unable to work and absent for three months, and during that time the employer pays all benefits on behalf of the employee and restores him to his same position, the employer should do the same for an employee who is unable to work due to pregnancy-related physical restrictions. The employer's obligation in this example does not apply to child care leave which does not involve physical restrictions on the employee's ability to work.

If an employer has a question regarding pregnancy leave, the employer should also consider the discussion elsewhere in this Guide which focuses on various leaves of absence–disability, personal, family and parental–and the potential for discrimination violations with respect to the terms and conditions under which such leaves are permitted.

ALCOHOL AND DRUG PROBLEMS IN THE WORKPLACE

ALCOHOLISM AND DRUG ADDICTION AS PROTECTED DISABILITIES

An individual with alcoholism or a drug addiction is protected under the Minnesota Human Rights Act as a "qualified disabled person" if he or she can, with reasonable accommodation, perform the essential functions of the job in question and does not constitute a direct threat to property or to the safety of others.[240] If the individual cannot perform the job (e.g. he or she does not come to work or is badly "hungover" at work) or if the individual is a threat to safety (e.g. his or her duties include driving a forklift), that individual is not a protected disabled person under Minnesota law and may be disciplined, up to and including termination. Disciplining or terminating an employee based on legitimate performance problems is not disability discrimination even if chemical dependency is the root cause of the performance problems. However, the employer must be careful in determining actual performance problems rather than mere suspicions that chemically dependent people make poor employees. All disciplinary actions should be imposed on employees in a uniform and non-discriminatory manner.

The problem employers often have with alcoholic or addicted employees is that the condition may be suspected but not proven. The employer runs a risk of defaming an employee when there is no proof of the addictive condition, such as may be established if the employer maintains a drug testing program (see below). In dealing with an employee suspected of alcoholism or addiction, it would not be defamatory to ask the employee whether his or her absenteeism, poor performance, etc. is caused by drinking (or other substance abuse), so long as such an inquiry is not communicated as a statement of fact to the employee or to any other person. It is acceptable to ask whether this is the problem and, if not, what the problem is, and offer the individual time off for treatment either on an in-patient or out-patient basis. The employer should not insist or require an employee to undergo chemical dependency treatment as a condition of continued employment. Minnesota's insurance statutes require that chemical dependency treatment be at least partially covered under most employer group health plans.[241]

The employer is advised to offer an employee with an abuse problem an opportunity for treatment or rehabilitation before taking any disciplinary action. The employer can require that treatment be at the employee's expense or under the group health plan; it need not pay for treatment unless it has done so for other employees. If the employee refuses to take advantage of this offer and the employee continues to perform poorly, absent any other legal restrictions, the employer should be able to take disciplinary action against such an employee. Any such action should be based on unacceptably poor performance, and not on the underlying condition, should be consistent with the employer's policies as set forth in the employee handbook or elsewhere, and should be based on the same policies applied to all employees. Because of the potential for liability based on defamation and disability discrimination, the employer is advised to seek the advice of legal counsel prior to counseling, disciplining, or terminating an employee suspected of substance abuse.

DRUG AND ALCOHOL TESTING IN THE WORKPLACE

A Minnesota employer may require its employees, as a condition of employment, to submit to a drug and alcohol test under certain circumstances.[242] All employees performing the same job must be subject to the drug and alcohol test. There must be a written policy which contains information required by the Minnesota drug testing statute. Each employee should receive a copy of the policy, and notice regarding the availability of copies of the policy should be posted in conspicuous places. Testing can occur only under the following circumstances:

- The employer has reasonable suspicion to believe that the employee:

    - Is under the influence of drugs or alcohol;

    - Has violated the employer's rules prohibiting the use, possession, sale or transfer of drugs or alcohol at work or on the employer's premises while operating the employer's vehicle, machinery or equipment;

    - Has sustained a personal injury or caused another employee to sustain a personal injury; or

    - Has caused a work-related accident or was operating vehicles or machinery involved in a work-related accident.

- Testing an employee without notice is permissible during and up to two years following the employee's completion of a drug or alcohol treatment program under an employee benefit plan or pursuant to a referral by the employer.

- A drug or alcohol test can be required as part of a routine physical exam, provided the test is required no more than once annually and employees have been given at least two weeks' written notice prior to the test.

- Random testing, without notice, may be conducted for employees in safety sensitive positions. A "safety sensitive" position is a job in which drug or alcohol impairment would threaten the health or safety of any person.

Drug and alcohol testing may not be required of employees other than under the circumstances listed above. The testing must be done by a laboratory which meets certain criteria described in the drug testing statute. Certain chain of custody and laboratory procedures must be followed.

The employee has the right to both explain a positive test and have a third test (after the required initial and confirmatory tests) conducted at his or her own expense.

Other than suspension for safety reasons during the testing process, an employer may not discharge or otherwise discipline an employee after his or her first positive testing incident (positive initial and confirmatory and, if requested, third tests) unless the employee is first offered an opportunity to go into treatment or rehabilitation and the employee either fails to complete or refuses to participate in the treatment program. Treatment need not be paid for by the employer; however, all or a portion of the treatment program will be covered under most group health insurance plans. The employer, after consulting with a certified chemical dependency counselor or physician, may determine the appropriate treatment program.

Following a second positive testing incident, the employee is subject to discipline, up to and including termination. A description of possible disciplinary action must be set forth in the policy. All information in an employee's personnel file involving drug and alcohol testing must be maintained in strictest confidence. Access to this information should be severely restricted within the company and should not be revealed to any person outside the company unless otherwise required by law or with the written consent of the employee.

Minnesota law has specific requirements with respect to testing procedures, including written notification to employees of test results and other procedures which must be followed by employers who have adopted drug testing policies. The law is comprehensive and is aimed at protection of both the employee and the employer.

If any adverse employment action is taken as a result of a drug or alcohol test, the employer has a responsibility under Minnesota law to notify the employee in writing of the reason for the decision within ten days of the date on which the decision is made.[243]

DRUG AND ALCOHOL POLICY

Even if an employer does not institute a drug and alcohol testing policy, the employer is well advised to put its employees on notice that it will not tolerate drug or alcohol use, sale, possession, or the like in the workplace, on work time or while operating company vehicles or machinery and that violations of the policy will result in termination of employment. Communication of such a policy to employees will put them on notice that they are subject to discharge for violating the policy. As discussed above, employers are advised to seek legal advice prior to counseling, disciplining or discharging employees for reasons relating to substance abuse, due to the potential liability for defamation and disability discrimination.

THE DRUG FREE WORKPLACE ACT
AND OTHER FEDERAL REQUIREMENTS

The Drug Free Workplace Act of 1988 is a federal law which requires that all businesses which have contracts with the federal government exceeding $100,000 must certify that they will maintain a drug free workplace.[244] The law requires that the employer notify employees of its drug free workplace policy. The policy must state that the unlawful manufacture, distribution, possession or use of a controlled substance is prohibited in the workplace. The employer must also establish a drug free awareness program to inform employees about the dangers of drug abuse, potential disciplinary actions for violations of the policy and available drug counseling and rehabilitation programs. Various agencies and departments of the federal government may impose additional requirements on government contractors.

The law also requires that any employee who is convicted of a criminal drug offense occurring in the workplace must notify the employer within five days after the conviction. The employer must notify the government contracting officer of the conviction within ten days after learning of the conviction. Within 30 days after receiving notice of the conviction, the employer must either discipline the convicted employee or require the employee to satisfactorily complete a drug treatment program. Any business which violates the Act risks losing its federal contract.

The Drug Free Workplace Act applies to drugs only and not to alcohol, but employers who are subject to the Act are strongly encouraged to prohibit alcohol as well as drugs in their policies. The Act does not require drug testing. Other federal rules and statutes, however, may have their own requirements with regard to drug and alcohol policies and testing. For example, employers with employees in positions regulated by the federal Department of Transportation (DOT) must conduct certain mandatory drug and alcohol testing under rules issued by the DOT and its operating administrations. Employees subject to DOT regulation include certain truck and bus drivers, workers involved in gas and pipeline operations, and airline and merchant marine personnel. The federal rules on drug and alcohol testing are detailed and complex in nature. For this reason, employers whose employees may be subject to DOT regulation should consult their legal counsel for assistance in complying with these rules.

OFF-DUTY DRUG AND ALCOHOL USE

Many employers would like to terminate the employment of an employee who is arrested for or convicted of an off-duty DUI, possession of narcotics, or other conduct the employer regards as unbecoming of its business or harmful to its reputation. Even though Minnesota is still an "at will" employment state, an employer will be best protected if its employment actions are reasonably based on performance at work and if the employee is on notice ahead of time that certain actions could result in discipline or discharge. Therefore, discipline or discharge of an employee for off-duty conduct should be related to the job and the workplace and should not occur unless there is no question that the employee committed harmful off-duty conduct. In addition, the employer's drug and alcohol policy (discussed above), should contain a provision which states that off-duty use or sale of drugs could result in adverse employment action if the off-duty conduct is harmful to the reputation of the employer, is related to the job which the employee is performing, or in some other way is not in the best interests of the employer. Note, however, that Minnesota law prohibits discipline or discharge of an employee based on the employee's off-duty use or enjoyment of "lawful consumable products," including alcohol and tobacco[245] (for a more detailed discussion of this law, see the section on smoking in this Guide).

SEARCHES

Like off-duty conduct, the issue of searches arises frequently in the drug and alcohol context. It also appears in the context of employee theft. Because this is an area loaded with potential liability in the areas of defamation, intentional or negligent infliction of emotional distress and other claims, employers should not conduct searches without first obtaining legal advice on this issue.

If searches are being considered, it is advisable for employers to have a distributed and acknowledged search policy, stating that searches are possible, that certain defined areas are subject to search and that employee cooperation with a search is a condition of employment.

AGE DISCRIMINATION

Minnesota law protects individuals who have attained the age of majority (18) from discrimination in the workplace based on age. Federal law, the Age Discrimination in Employment Act ("ADEA"), protects persons age 40 or older from age discrimination by employers with 20 or more employees. An employer who is not covered by ADEA may require an employee who has attained age 70 to retire. If such an employer adopts a policy of mandatorily retiring employees at age 70, the employer must post a notice to that effect which has been approved by the Minnesota Commissioner of Labor. If an employer intends to terminate an employee who is 65 years or older but not yet age 70 on the ground that the employee can no longer meet the requirements of the job, the employer must give the employee 30 days' advance notice of intention to terminate the employee's employment.[246]

Please note that mandatory retirement at age 70, even though permitted under Minnesota law, is a violation of the federal ADEA, which applies to any employer who has 20 or more employees during each working day in each of 20 or more calendar weeks in the current or preceding calendar year.[247] Part-time and temporary employees count in determining whether the employer meets the 20 employee threshold.

The ADEA protects any individual age 40 or over from adverse employment action based on age. Therefore, for employers with 20 or more employees, an employee age 40 or older can never be terminated because of age so long as that person is able to perform the job. Termination of an employee over 40, therefore, must occur for performance or another nondiscriminatory reason such as a reduction in force. Note that individuals over age 40 may bring age discrimination claims under the ADEA even if they are replaced by people younger than them who are also over age 40.[248]

Although age discrimination is generally thought of in terms of older workers, Minnesota employers must be mindful that they may not discriminate against younger persons on the basis of age. For example, an employer should not refuse to hire a 19 year old for a position merely because the individual is perceived as "too young." The employer may, however, refuse to hire a 19 year old because that person does not possess the necessary skills to perform the job.

Both federal and Minnesota law provide exceptions to the prohibition on adverse employment action due to age. For example:

- In rare cases (e.g., in some situations, pilots, police officers or fire fighters), age may be a bona fide occupational qualification and, therefore, termination based on age may be permissible.

- When executives or high policy making individuals between ages 65 and 70 are terminated and provided with an annual retirement benefit of $27,000 (Minnesota law) or $44,000 (ADEA) for life, the termination may be permissible. The rules relating to this exception are complex.

- Other exceptions involve providing lower employee benefits to older employees based purely on cost, i.e., the cost of the benefit for the older employee is roughly the same as the cost for the younger employee but the older employee is entitled to a lesser benefit because of his or her age and life expectancy.

The use of any exceptions to either Minnesota or ADEA age discrimination prohibitions should be carefully planned with legal counsel.

When terminating an older employee, the employer should not mention the advisability or attractiveness of retirement, the need for "new blood" or the like in any discussions with the employee or with others. Although some courts have disregarded isolated stray remarks about an employee's age, such remarks may infer an intent to discriminate, especially if made by a member of management or in the context of some adverse employment action against an older worker. The employer should never tell the employee that he or she is being forced or "asked" to retire, except under one of the very limited exceptions discussed above. Any such remarks could be used as evidence of age discrimination. The age factor should be eliminated in all discussions which relate to an individual's employment unless the individual raises the subject, e.g., by asking questions relating to retirement benefits.

EARLY RETIREMENT PROGRAMS

Employers who are planning to reduce their workforce may legally institute early retirement programs which offer incentives to certain groups of employees who wish to take the opportunity to retire early. These programs are permissible so long as the choice to accept or reject the early retirement offer is truly voluntary and the employee is in no worse a position than other similarly situated employees if he or she does not elect the early retirement option. Employees must be given adequate time (a minimum of 45 days) and opportunity to become informed as to the advantages and disadvantages of accepting the early retirement offer and to consult with legal counsel.

Incentives often include benefits such as 100 percent vesting in the employer's retirement plan, cash payments based upon years of service, and continued group health insurance coverage. Because of complex issues relating to these programs, such as coverage of the program under the Employee Retirement Income Security Act and the danger of inadvertently providing greater benefits to the younger members of the targeted group, an early retirement program should be undertaken only with the advice of legal counsel.

WAIVER OF RIGHTS UNDER THE
AGE DISCRIMINATION LAWS

Employers who are terminating the employment of older employees often enter into settlement agreements with these employees in which the employer provides benefits to the employee in return for the employee's release of his or her claims against the employer. The release usually focuses on waiving rights that the employee may otherwise have to bring claims of age discrimination under the Minnesota Human Rights Act or the ADEA. Such releases will usually be upheld if the agreement contains specific language notifying the employee of his or her 15-day right of rescission under the Minnesota Human Rights Act and/or the 7-day right of rescission under the ADEA, as applicable.[249]

Under the ADEA, the employer must provide the employee with at least 21 days to consider an individual agreement and to consult with legal counsel before signing the agreement, and another seven days to rescind the agreement after having signed it. The employer may revoke its settlement offer during the 21 day review period before the employee accepts. If the waiver is requested in connection with an exit incentive program such as an early retirement program discussed in the previous section, the employer is subject to additional specific notice requirements and the 21 day review period for the employee is increased to 45 days. Be aware that when an employer requests waivers from two or more employees, it may be considered an exit incentive type program under the ADEA and that additional information must be included in the release document in order for it to be enforceable.

To be enforceable, an agreement which contains a release of age claims in exchange for benefits must describe in clear and understandable language the time periods for review and rescission, the specific rights that the employee is waiving, advice as to the employee's right to consult with an attorney and the fact that the agreement does not waive rights of the employee which arise after the agreement is signed.[250] These requirements are strictly interpreted and the EEOC from time to time issues regulations and Guidance documents describing its view on the requirements of a knowing and voluntary waiver of ADEA claims. In fact, a release of age discrimination claims that does not satisfy all of the statutory requirements is not an effective waiver of claims and does not prevent the assertion of an ADEA claim even if the employee signs the waiver and release agreement it and keeps the money or other consideration offered in connection with the release of claims.[251] Therefore, these (as well as all other) release agreements should be implemented only with the advice of legal counsel.

Also, there must be no hint of coercion or undue pressure on the employee. The amount of consideration (benefits) provided generally depends upon the employee's salary, the length of employment and other like factors.

SEX DISCRIMINATION

DEFINITION

Employers may not make employment decisions based on an applicant's or employee's sex (gender) or discriminate against one sex with respect to the terms and conditions of employment. Claims in this area arise out of allegations that an employer has engaged in discriminatory job assignments, classifications, layoffs, pay and promotion practices due to sex, or stereotypical assumptions based on gender. Also, work rules that are not discriminatory on their face but adversely affect one sex are lawful only if "manifestly related to the job" or if they "significantly further an important business purpose," such as height requirements for flight attendants.[252] Some other potential sex discrimination claims include the following:

FETAL PROTECTION

Some employers have, in the past, restricted the jobs available to pregnant women and women of childbearing age because they believed that those jobs may be harmful to an existing or future fetus. Such "fetal protection" policies have been declared unlawful as discriminatory against women on the basis of sex.[253] Fetal protection policies will be permissible only under extremely limited circumstances, and any employer considering such a policy is urged to seek legal counsel and the expert advice of an occupational safety expert. Employers whose employees work in such potentially hazardous positions should also seek legal advice as to steps that they can take to avoid liability in such situations.

MALE SEX DISCRIMINATION

As state and federal civil rights laws have opened up new opportunities for women in the workplace, women are now advancing into supervisory roles and constitute a majority in some workplaces. In addition, males are more frequently working at traditionally female jobs, such as nursing. Consequently, there has been an increase in claims of sex discrimination against males and even sexual harassment against males. Employers should be aware of these potential claims.

EQUAL PAY FOR EQUAL WORK

In addition to the prohibition against sex discrimination set forth in the federal Equal Pay Act[254] and in the discrimination laws, Minnesota's Equal Pay for Equal Work law[255] prohibits employers from paying different wages to employees of the opposite sex for equal work on jobs which require the same skills, effort, and responsibility, and which are performed under similar working conditions. Differences in payment may be made pursuant to a seniority system, a merit system, or any other system which measures earnings by quantity or quality of production, or any other factor except for sex.[256] Employers are also prohibited from retaliating against employees who have filed complaints or have testified in investigations pursuant to the Equal Pay for Equal Work law.

LILLY LEDBETTER FAIR PAY ACT

On January 29, 2009, the Lilly Ledbetter Fair Pay Act became law. This law extends the statutory time limit for filing pay discrimination claims, declaring that each paycheck following an initial discriminatory pay decision creates a new unlawful employment practice. This means that employees can recover back pay for up to two years preceding the filing of a discrimination claim and it significantly extends the time period during which employees may file wage discrimination claims. This may also permit retirees to sue for pay-related discrimination if they currently receive a pension or health care that may have been affected by discrimination. The effect of this law will be seen as court decisions refine its application in the future.

SEXUAL HARASSMENT

DEFINITION

Sexual harassment is a form of sex discrimination. It exists in the workplace where an employee is subjected to unwelcome advances, suggestive comments, or physical contact of a sexual nature which create an intimidating, hostile or offensive working environment. Sexual harassment also exists if any employment decision affecting an employee is related in any way to the employee's participation in, or rejection of, conduct of a sexual nature. The perpetrators of sexual harassment may be supervisors, co-workers, or even non-employees such as customers, vendors, and others who come into contact with the company's employees. Employers may be held liable if they are aware an employee is subject to sexual harassment by employees or non-employees, yet fail to take timely and appropriate actions to protect their employees.[257]

Sexual harassment cases have involved allegations of a man harassing a woman, a woman harassing a man, and people of the same sex harassing one another.[258]

POLICY

Every employer should have a written policy which (i) defines sexual harassment and other forms of unlawful harassment in the workplace, (ii) emphatically states that the employer will not tolerate harassment, (iii) encourages anyone who believes he or she is a victim of harassment to come forward and file a complaint, and (iv) assures a prompt and confidential investigation and resolution of the problem. A sexual harassment policy is often part of a general harassment policy, which prohibits harassment toward employees on the basis of all legally protected classifications, including, e.g., age, disability and religion. A growing number of employers have broadened their sexual harassment policies to prohibit all types of unlawful harassment, and a number of employers have adopted further policies that call upon all employees to treat each other with dignity and respect.

The policy should describe the various individuals to whom harassment complaints can be directed, and it should assure the complaining employee that there will be no retaliation as a result of bringing such a complaint. The policy should set out some general procedures which will be followed when a complaint is brought. The employer is advised to provide every employee with a copy of the policy (e.g., through an employee handbook) and to have employee meetings from time to time to ensure that potential victims understand that they need not tolerate harassment and to warn potential offenders that they are subject to discipline and discharge for violating the policy. Small employers may find that informal complaint procedures are effective and larger employers may wish to adopt more formalized reporting and resolution procedures. However, regardless of the details, it is critical that all employers adopt and communicate the essential elements of a harassment policy.

Federal and state law regarding sexual harassment provides employers a major incentive for adopting and distributing a policy against sexual harassment. The United States Supreme Court has ruled that employers are (1) always liable for harassment committed by supervisors that leads to a tangible adverse effect such as termination or demotion, and (2) also liable for supervisor harassment with less tangible harm unless they can show that they tried to prevent the harassment by adopting a policy and took appropriate corrective action when learning of the harassment.[259] Similarly, the Minnesota Legislature has indicated that Minnesota law concerning sexual harassment should be interpreted consistently with federal law. Moreover, the Minnesota Court of Appeals has cautioned: "[c]ompanies that fail to institute such polices will naturally find themselves vulnerable to the likelihood that knowledge [of the harassment] will be imputed to them," thereby increasing the risk that the employer will be liable for the harassment.[260]

INVESTIGATION

Harassment complaints should be followed by a thorough investigation of the complaint. It is essential that the investigation be conducted immediately by a competent, disinterested investigator (either a company employee trained to do such investigations or an outside professional). Promises of complete confidentiality to complainants may limit an employer's ability to take adequate timely and appropriate action in response to a complaint and do not remove the employer's legal obligation to take such action.

One person at the company should be in charge of such complaints (although employees should be encouraged to bring their complaints to the attention of any management member with whom they may feel more comfortable) and this person should receive all of the details of the complaint (who, what, when, where, witnesses) and have a discussion with the accused to get his or her side of the story. The company should not prejudge the problem before doing a thorough investigation, it should keep the entire matter as confidential as possible, and it should take great care not to defame (wrongly accuse) the accused or any other individual in the process of conducting the investigation.

DISCIPLINE AND RESOLUTION

If the employer determines that harassment did occur, then the harasser must be disciplined. The extent of the discipline should depend upon the severity of the offense. A warning not to repeat the behavior may be appropriate in some situations while discharge may be appropriate in others. Sensitivity training, suspension and transfer are other options. However, the complainant should not be transferred unless he or she requests the transfer or agrees with it. A transfer against the wishes of the complainant could constitute unlawful retaliation.

If there is no proof of harassment following the investigation, the employer may not take disciplinary action against the accused. All parties can be reminded of the company's policy and to come forward if any other problems occur.

FOLLOW-UP AND RETALIATION

The employer should follow up after any harassment incident to make sure–if the investigation resulted in a finding of harassment and the harasser is still employed–that no further harassment is taking place. In addition, it is extremely important for the employer to ensure that the complainant is not subject to retaliatory action of any kind following the complaint.

ROMANCE IN THE WORKPLACE

Employers who are faced with a romantic relationship between employees (often supervisor and subordinate) should be aware of potential liabilities arising out of these relationships, over and above the morale problems of other employees, drain on productivity, and gossip. If the relationship sours, for example, the subordinate may try to claim that the supervisor was pressuring the subordinate into the relationship in exchange for promotions. Harassment claims also may arise if one party is trying to break off the relationship and the other party is not accepting the breakup. In addition, other employees in the workplace may feel disadvantaged in their work because they are not romantically involved with the boss. These issues could develop into sexual harassment claims against the employer.

An employer can try to protect itself in this situation by talking with each party separately to assure that the relationship is mutual and warning supervisors in such relationships against favoritism. The employer also can protect itself by being prepared to respond promptly to complaints or signs of harassment. Since this is such a sensitive area and management is typically reluctant to intrude into the privacy of employees, this problem should be approached and handled carefully, with advice of legal counsel. Similarly, employers should exercise caution about expressing discontent or interfering in any way with an employee's relationships outside the workplace, in light of various privacy laws.

SEXUAL ORIENTATION DISCRIMINATION

Unlike federal law, the Minnesota Human Rights Act includes sexual orientation as a protected category.[261] Sexual orientation discrimination (sometimes known as "affectional preference" discrimination) is also prohibited under Minneapolis and St. Paul city ordinances.[262]

The Human Rights Act defines sexual orientation as "having or being perceived as having an emotional, physical or sexual attachment to another person without regard to the sex of that person or having or being perceived as having an orientation for such attachment, or having or being perceived as having a self-image or identity not traditionally associated with one's biological maleness or femaleness." This definition does not require employers to provide restrooms to transgender persons based upon their self image; employers may restrict such facilities according to biological gender.[263] "Sexual orientation" does not include a physical or sexual attachment to children by an adult.[264]

Unlike some of the other protected categories, several exceptions apply to sexual orientation as a protected category. For example, religious associations are not prohibited from taking any actions on matters related to sexual orientation and employment.[265] In addition, non-public service organizations that primarily serve minors do not commit unfair discriminatory employment practices if they have qualifications for employees or volunteers based on sexual orientation.[266] Finally, nothing in this category is to be construed to authorize or permit the use of numerical goals or quotas, or other types of affirmative action programs, with respect to homosexuality or bisexuality in the administration or enforcement of this category.

MARITAL STATUS DISCRIMINATION

Under the Minnesota Human Rights Act, an employer may not discriminate against an applicant or an employee because of that individual's marital status.[267] An individual's marital status includes whether that individual is single, married, remarried, divorced, separated or a surviving spouse. The prohibition against marital status discrimination also specifically includes protection against discrimination on the basis of the identity, situation, actions or beliefs of a spouse or former spouse.[268]

For example, an employer may not have a policy of not hiring spouses of current employees. If the spouse of an employee is politically active in an organization with which the employer does not agree, the employer may not fire its employee because it does not like the opinions of the employee's spouse. Another example of marital status discrimination in Minnesota would be where the employee is transferred to another city and the employee's spouse refuses to move to the other city. The employer may not discharge the employee because his or her spouse refuses to move to the new location.[269]

RACE DISCRIMINATION

Racial or minority discrimination, including discrimination based upon an individual's membership in a particular ethnic group, can be manifested by harassing, hostile, or intimidating remarks or behavior, unequal opportunity in the hiring process, lower wages, fewer opportunities for promotion or more unfavorable working conditions. An example of race discrimination is the unequal application of employment practices, such as a situation where only minority applicants are subjected to background checks for criminal records or credit history. To avoid such problems, employers are urged to adopt anti-harassment policies, to diligently publicize them to employees and to enforce them. Employers should also apply discipline and other working policies uniformly and consciously extend work opportunities to minority group members, where they are qualified.

National origin discrimination involves many of the same issues, as well as issues involving language and the ability of the applicant or employee to communicate clearly with customers. Employers are encouraged to seek the advice of legal counsel before making employment decisions based upon language, in order to assure that an ability to clearly communicate in English is a bona fide occupational qualification.

RELIGIOUS DISCRIMINATION

Both federal and Minnesota law prohibit employment discrimination on account of the religious beliefs of an applicant or employee. Employers should permit employees to practice their religious faith at work to the extent that it does not interfere with job requirements or the job performance of other employees. A number of employers provide space for employees to pray or study religious texts during break times or outside of working hours. Other employers permit exceptions to their dress code or grooming policy based on religion. However, unlike the disability discrimination laws that require employers to provide reasonable accommodation, federal and Minnesota statutes pertaining to the accommodation of religion have been interpreted to require accommodation only where the accommodation would create minimal hardship for the employer. For example, changing work shift schedules to permit an employee to observe his or her Sabbath is not required where such changes would disrupt the employer's normal operations. Nor is an employer expected to permit proselytizing at work where other employees object to or are uncomfortable with such activity.

RETALIATION

Employers should be careful to avoid taking adverse employment action against any employee who complains about discrimination or about any other violation of the law involving the workplace. Minnesota law protects such employees by assuring that "blowing the whistle" on illegal acts[270] or exercising certain rights will not cost them their jobs or make their working environment difficult. Examples of such protected employees include those who complain about any form of discrimination or OSHA violations, or those who file workers' compensation claims, ask to see their personnel files, or exercise their right to take parental leave. Reports concerning the employee's good faith belief of unlawful conduct may be made about any law, not just laws that reflect some important public policy.[271] The reports can be made internally to management or externally to some government official. In addition, the Sarbanes-Oxley Act is a federal law that prohibits public companies from retaliating or discriminating against employees who provide information, assist in investigations, file, testify or otherwise participate in proceedings concerning the financial affairs of the company. A list of some of the laws which provide specific protection against retaliation appears in the section of this Guide on terminations.

The prohibition against retaliation does not mean that an employer may never discipline an employee who complains or exercises certain legal rights. Rather, the discipline may not be a result of the complaint. Adverse action taken after a complaint, particularly where there is no record of disciplinary action before the complaint, will appear to be retaliation.

Employers should alert supervisory personnel of the protected status of these employees so the employees will not be subjected to harassment, demotions, discipline or other forms of retaliation as a result of their complaints or the exercise of their rights.

A decision issued by the U.S. Supreme Court significantly expands the scope of potential retaliation claims and, in doing so, underscores the importance for employers of ensuring they have adequate procedures in place to prevent retaliation against employees who complain of discrimination.[272] The Court determined that federal anti-discrimination law is not restricted to harms that are related to employment or occur at the workplace. In a departure from previous rulings, the Court stated that events occurring outside the workplace may support a claim for illegal retaliation. Under this decision, an individual must show that the employer's action would have been "materially adverse to a reasonable employee or applicant."[273] To satisfy this requirement, a complaining employee must demonstrate that the alleged act of retaliation "could well dissuade a reasonable worker from making or supporting a charge of discrimination."[274]

Retaliation is a separate violation under most laws. For example, if an employee complains of sexual harassment and, as a result, is demoted or otherwise subjected to adverse employment action, even if there is no validity to the sexual harassment claim, the employee may have an actionable claim for retaliation.

Employers should also keep in mind that the law protects employees who in good faith allege that they have been the subject of discrimination, harassment, or some other unlawful action. It is illegal to retaliate against such individuals through termination, demotion, or assignment of undesirable job duties on account of their complaints or allegations. The anti-retaliation provisions of federal law also protect a company's former employees.[275] Thus, providing a negative reference or otherwise interfering with former employees' attempts to find other employment because they previously made allegations of an unlawful employment practice is forbidden.

SMOKING

LIMITING OR PROHIBITING SMOKING IN THE WORKPLACE

Employers may not refuse to hire an applicant because he or she is a smoker. This policy has been reinforced by the Minnesota Lawful Consumable Products Act, which protects certain off-duty conduct, including use of tobacco.[276]

Minnesota's "Freedom to Breathe Act" prohibits smoking in virtually all indoor public places and all places of employment.[277] The ban covers "any indoor area at which two or more individuals perform any type of a service" for payment and includes hallways, restrooms, elevators, lounges, auditoriums, employee cafeterias, and other shared office areas (e.g. areas containing photocopying equipment).[278] The ban also includes vehicles "used in whole or in part for work purposes . . . during hours of operation if more than one person is present."[279] Private residences also may fall under the ban if the area is used "exclusively and regularly" as a place of business with one or more on-site employees, or if the homeowner uses the area "exclusively and regularly" to meet with patients, clients, or customers.

Significant exceptions to the ban include private places (e.g. private homes, private residences, and private automobiles when not used as a "place of employment"); tobacco products shops; cabs of heavy commercial vehicles; farm vehicles and construction equipment; and family farms employing two or fewer non-family members.[280]

The law tasks employers with making "reasonable efforts" to prevent smoking in their place of employment.[281] Specifically, employers are required to:[282]

- Post appropriate signs;

- Ask persons who smoke in prohibited areas to refrain from smoking and to leave if they refuse to do so;

- Use lawful methods consistent with handling disorderly persons or trespassers for any person who refused to comply after being asked to leave the premises;

- Refrain from providing ashtrays and other smoking equipment; and

- Refuse to serve noncompliant persons.

Employers should note that knowingly failing to comply with enforcement of the ban will subject them to a petty misdemeanor charge.[283] The law specifically prevents employers from discharging, refusing to hire, penalizing, discriminating against, or retaliating against an employee, applicant, or customer in any manner because the individual exercises their "right to a smoke-free environment."[284] Finally, under the law, local governments retain the authority to adopt and enforce more stringent measures.[285] Employers should consult legal counsel where a local government has acted to regulate smoking in the workplace to ensure compliance with all applicable regulations.

In implementing the smoking ban, employers should also be mindful of Minnesota's Lawful Consumable Products Act, which is discussed below.

THE LAWFUL CONSUMABLE PRODUCTS ACT

The Minnesota Lawful Consumable Products Act, regarded by some people as a smoker's rights law, prohibits employers from refusing to hire an applicant or from disciplining an employee because that person engages in the use or enjoyment of lawful consumable products, if the consumption takes place off the employer's premises during non-working hours.[286] "Lawful consumable products" are products whose use or enjoyment is lawful, including food, alcoholic or non-alcoholic beverages, and tobacco. An employer may, however, restrict the use of lawful consumable products by employees during non-working hours if the restriction relates to a bona fide occupational requirement, is necessary to avoid a conflict or an apparent conflict of interest with any of the employee's job responsibilities, or is part of a chemical dependency or treatment program. Employers may also make distinctions between employees as to cost of insurance or health coverage based upon the employee's use of lawful consumable products, so long as the difference in costs reflects the actual different costs to the employer. An employer violating the statute may be liable for lost wages and benefits, along with costs and attorneys' fees.

POLYGRAPH TESTING

Under state and federal law, employers may not, directly or indirectly, request or require an applicant or current employee to take a polygraph, voice stress analysis, or any other test purporting to test the honesty of the applicant or employee.[287] This prohibition relates to tests which measure physiological changes and does not apply to written honesty tests.[288] Under Minnesota law, an employee may request a polygraph test. If an employee makes such a request, the employer or agent administering the test still must inform the employee that the test is voluntary. The employer is then prohibited from disclosing that any employee or applicant has taken a polygraph test and may not disclose the results of the test except to persons authorized by the employee to receive the results.[289]

GARNISHMENT OF WAGES

If certain statutory requirements are met, an employer who receives a garnishment notice concerning an employee is required to garnish the appropriate amount from the employee's wages.[290] The maximum amount which may be garnished from an employee's wages is the lesser of 25 percent of the employee's disposable earnings or the amount by which the debtor's disposable earnings exceed the product of 40 times the federal minimum wage times the number of work weeks in the pay period.[291] Special rules may apply where the underlying judgment is for child support. "Disposable earnings" is defined as the earnings remaining after deduction from those earnings of amounts required by law to be withheld.

An employer is prohibited by law from retaliating against any employee due to garnishment.[292]

EMPLOYEE HANDBOOKS

Employee handbooks can be an efficient and effective way for employers to communicate their workplace rules to employees, so that employees will be on notice of the rules with which they are expected to comply. When an employer's rules are clearly communicated to employees in writing, it is difficult for an employee to profess ignorance of those rules. The employee is in fact much less likely to violate rules when the employee knows what the rules are and the consequences of violations. At the same time, if employers expect employees to follow their rules, employees (and courts) will expect employers to honor any commitments which they make to employees in handbooks. As a general guideline, employers adopting and disseminating employee handbooks should consider including the following:

- Introduction, which includes language indicating that the handbook is not an employment contract, that employment is at-will (meaning that either the employer or the employee can terminate the employment relationship at any time, with or without notice, for any lawful reason), that the employer's at-will policy can be overridden only by a written contract signed by the president of the employer, and that the current handbook supersedes any prior handbooks or policies.

- Acknowledgment, stating that the employee understands and agrees to abide by the handbook's rules and policies and that employment is at-will. The employer should give the acknowledgment form to the employee at hire (or upon adoption of the handbook), have the employee sign and date the form after the employee reviews the handbook, and return it to the employee's personnel file.

- Notice of the employer's right to revise or rescind the handbook at any time, and language indicating that the current handbook supersedes prior handbook language.

- Harassment policy, which includes general procedures for prompt and objective investigation of harassment complaints, the employer representative to whom complaints should be directed, and assurances of no retaliation.

- Equal employment opportunity policy.

- Vacation and sick leave policies. Note that Family and Medical Leave Act policies, discussed elsewhere in this Guide, are required to be set forth in detail in an employer's handbook if the handbook is available to employees and the employer is subject to the FMLA.

- Policy regarding authorization for overtime work.

- Policy regarding prompt reporting of workplace injuries.

- Absenteeism policy, which may include, depending upon the size of the employer, and, as appropriate, leave policies (personal, medical, family, parental, funeral, military, voting).

The employer may also elect to include the following:

- Drug and alcohol policy, including testing if applicable.

- No smoking policy.

- Confidentiality policy, prohibiting disclosure of the employer's trade secrets and proprietary information.

- Voice-mail, e-mail, and computer policies which describe the employer's right of access, make clear employees have no expectation to privacy in using these systems and prohibit improper use of these facilities by employees.

- No solicitation/distribution policy.

- A brief description of employee benefits, referring the employee to the Summary Plan Description for each benefit plan.

There are many other possibilities, depending upon the needs of the workplace and the rules and commitments which the employer wishes to communicate. A number of employers have included provisions in their employee handbooks requiring employees to arbitrate any dispute regarding their employment or to participate in some type of mediation process before asserting a claim with a court or administrative agency. Arbitration tends to be faster and less expensive than litigation in court. Mediation is a process of discussion in which a neutral third party helps parties to find some common ground to avoid or resolve a dispute.

The United States Supreme Court has ruled that agreements requiring employees to arbitrate employment disputes, including discrimination claims, are valid and enforceable.[293] Such agreements should be knowingly made by employees and the procedures should not deprive employees of substantive rights such as the ability to recover the same types of damages that could be recovered through litigation. Employers that wish to consider requiring all employees to sign arbitration agreements as a condition of employment should consult with legal counsel regarding the proper implementation of such agreements, particularly with respect to current employees. Employers should keep in mind that the existence of a mandatory arbitration agreement with a particular employee will not prevent the EEOC from bringing a lawsuit on behalf of that employee seeking remedies for that employee specifically or other employees generally.[294] Employers should also note that proceedings brought under the Minnesota Human Rights Act are exclusive while pending and that arbitration cannot be compelled during that period of time.[295]

The legal problems that employers experience with employee handbooks relate primarily to handbook commitments which employers make to their employees that they then fail to honor. Under Minnesota law, a commitment communicated to an employee in a handbook may constitute a contract and breach of this contract could result in liability for the employer if the employee sustains damages as a result of the breach.[296] To avoid this liability, the employer should consider excluding items such as the following from their handbooks:

- Progressive discipline procedures or promises regarding the disciplinary process. While an employer may choose to list general guidelines of discipline and/or unacceptable behavior, the employer should retain its full discretion to take whatever action it considers necessary and appropriate under the circumstances with respect to any disciplinary or performance issue.

- Any other promises which, if not honored, could give rise to liability, such as a promise to provide annual performance reviews or to hire from within.

Binding contracts which the employer may make also arise in offer letters, memoranda, oral promises and consistent customary practices, which could constitute implied contracts. An employer is free to make any commitments to an individual employee or to its employees as a whole which it believes will be beneficial to the company and the employees, recognizing that those commitments may constitute legal contracts which, if not honored, could result in legal liability. Legal counsel should review handbooks to ensure that the employer is not making written promises in the handbook that it is unwilling or unable to keep. Likewise, employers should consult legal counsel regarding the desirability of a handbook as opposed to a more limited set of written policies.

PROHIBITION AGAINST REPRISALS FOR REFUSING TO MAKE CHARITABLE CONTRIBUTIONS

Employers are prohibited from retaliating against employees who decline to contribute to charities or community organizations.[297] Under the statute, "reprisal" means any form of discipline, intimidation, harassment or threat, or any penalty regarding the employee's wages, terms or conditions of employment.

UNION ORGANIZATION AND COLLECTIVE BARGAINING

In general, issues arising when employees are represented by a collective bargaining agent are beyond the scope of this Guide. Employers facing such issues are advised to seek the advice of legal counsel familiar with federal and state labor laws. The discussion here is limited to a few issues which commonly arise when a bargaining unit is soliciting employees.

SOLICITATION/DISTRIBUTION RULES

An employer (including supervisors and managers) may not discriminate against or coerce its employees to join or not to join a labor organization.[298] Generally, an employer may not prohibit verbal solicitation of employees by other employees during non-work time and may not prohibit written solicitation in non-work areas during non-work time. Whether an employer can bar distribution of written materials in the work area during non-work time would depend upon considerations such as littering, interfering with production and the like.

Pursuant to a "no-access rule" which has been validly published and uniformly enforced, an employer may prohibit access by any outsiders to all working areas.

The rules stated above are general guidelines, but there are many exceptions to the general rules. Each case is fact specific. Employers are strongly encouraged to consult with legal counsel before adopting and publishing a no-solicitation/no-distribution rule. Improper implementation of such a rule may itself be a violation of the National Labor Relations Act.

EMPLOYEE FREE CHOICE ACT

The Employee Free Choice Act (EFCA) is proposed federal legislation that would amend the National Labor Relations Act, making significant changes to the union certification and collective bargaining processes. The proposed law would allow unions to be certified based on employees' signed authorization cards, in lieu of NLRB-conducted secret ballot elections, would authorize an arbitrator to impose the terms of a collective bargaining agreement for two years if an employer and union cannot agree on those terms, and would increase penalties for unfair labor practices committed by employers. Such legislation, if passed, will likely trigger a constitutional challenge and its final outcome is uncertain at the time this Guide is published.

WORKPLACE RULES

Employers are advised to establish workplace rules and to communicate these rules to employees. Some examples of workplace rules and effective methods of communication are set forth below.

- Certain posters are required to be posted in the workplace in conspicuous places. Information regarding the posters may be obtained by calling (651) 284-5005 (Minnesota Department of Labor and Industry) or (612) 370-3371 (Federal Department of Labor). Some examples of required posters are the Fair Labor Standards Act poster, the Minnesota Minimum Wage and Overtime poster, the Minnesota OSHA poster, the Equal Opportunity in Employment poster, and the Minnesota Unemployment poster.

- Written benefit information, including HIPAA and COBRA health insurance continuation rights and retirement and welfare plan summary plan descriptions, should be given to employees individually when they become eligible for the particular benefit.

- Employee handbooks (discussed in the Employee Handbooks section of this Guide) which set forth the rules for attendance, vacation, sick days, etc. are an effective means of communicating workplace rules to employees. Such handbooks should avoid making any contractual commitments to employees, while at the same time putting them on notice of the conduct and responsibilities which are required of them in the workplace. If you decide to provide employees a handbook, it should be reviewed by legal counsel before distribution.

- Some employers do not distribute a copy of the handbook to each employee but instead keep a few copies around the workplace which are available for review by employees on an ongoing basis. Such practice is not advisable, because of the risk that some employees may not review it. A handbook is easiest to update when kept in loose leaf form so that pages can be replaced as the employer's policies change or the law changes. Each time a change is made to the handbook, employees should be notified of the change by memorandum. Limited distribution of the handbook does not alter the need for careful drafting and for review by legal counsel.

- Various policies can be handed out to employees in memorandum form or can be incorporated into the handbook. Examples of such policies include attendance, smoking, drug and alcohol (with or without testing), and sexual harassment.

- All memoranda to employees should be handled by one person who understands the commitments which the employer is and is not willing to make to its employees. An employer should direct its supervisory and management personnel not to make commitments of any kind without prior approval, including both written and oral commitments or promises regarding the terms of employment.

- Rules and performance expectations can also be communicated through periodic employee meetings and performance reviews. All such meetings and discussions with employees should be documented and maintained in the employee's personnel file.

PROHIBITING WEAPONS IN THE WORKPLACE

Companies that wish to prohibit weapons, including handguns, on their premises should develop and implement clear policies. For employees, this should entail a written workplace violence prevention policy that prohibits employees from carrying, possessing, or using firearms while on company premises or while acting in the course and scope of employment. The policy should make clear that it applies to all employees, even those who may have a valid permit to carry a handgun. The company should also consider having the policy remind the employees of the company's search and inspection policy and the procedures for reporting threats of violence.

For visitors, the company should implement a policy whereby visitors are notified upon entry to the premises of the company's prohibition on weapons in its facility. Employers are advised to review their policies and procedures with legal counsel to ensure compliance with applicable law.

DISCIPLINE

Supervisors should conduct regular performance reviews. These reviews should be honest, suggest improvements, and give the employee an opportunity to respond in writing if he or she disagrees.

DISCRIMINATORY DISCIPLINE

Supervisors must apply standards of performance uniformly to all employees. For example, tardiness should not be tolerated from female employees when male employees are subject to reprimand or demerits for the same offense. Discriminatory remarks should not be made either verbally or in writing in any performance review. In one highly publicized case,[299] for example, a female accountant's male supervisors noted in her file that she should dress more femininely, wear more jewelry, and avoid profanity (although it was tolerated from male employees). She was denied partnership based on those sexually stereotyped comments and later successfully sued her employer. These types of remarks constitute sex discrimination and should not be tolerated.

DEFAMATION IN THE DISCIPLINARY PROCESS

Anyone writing performance reviews or any other notations in an employee's file should avoid defamatory remarks. Comments and criticisms should be limited to those which can be factually documented unless the notation clearly states that an allegation has been made but not proven. Access to employee personnel files should be severely restricted to only the person or persons who have an absolute need to know, usually the personnel director or person acting in that capacity. The employer should not make any announcements which could be defamatory before any groups of employees or other individuals, and should not make any comments whatsoever during or following the investigation of misconduct complaints (e.g., sexual harassment, theft, drugs). The employer should take care not to embarrass or humiliate an employee in the investigatory, disciplinary or termination process.

CONTRACTUAL COMMITMENTS IN THE DISCIPLINARY PROCESS

Employers should avoid committing themselves orally or in writing (such as in an employee handbook) to follow any particular pattern of discipline, such as "an employee will not be discharged before receiving three written warnings." The employer should retain the right to take whatever disciplinary action it determines is appropriate under the circumstances.

Similarly, an employer should not commit either orally or in writing to act "fairly" because that term could be interpreted in a variety of ways. In practice, however, employers should strive to act fairly, treat similarly situated employees similarly, and to give employees advance notice of performance deficiencies and the opportunity to improve.

ATTENDANCE

Employers are advised to notify their employees of their attendance, absenteeism and tardiness policies, and the disciplinary consequences which will flow from a violation of these rules. Again, this notification can be included in the employee handbook or in memorandum form. Employees should understand that they are required to appear at work at a certain hour and to stay until a certain hour and that excessive absenteeism or tardiness for any reason could result in termination. Courts have repeatedly held that regular and reliable attendance is an essential function of virtually every job and that past attendance is a legitimate, non-discriminatory reason for adverse employment action. However, the employer must enforce attendance policies uniformly, and it should document all incidents of tardiness or absenteeism.

Employees should be required to promptly notify their supervisors personally on each day that they will miss work (except with respect to long term leaves of absence). Some employers have advised their employees that if they do not show up for work or call in for two or three days in a row, they will be deemed to have voluntarily terminated their employment. Employers should keep in mind that such inflexible policies may conflict with employees' rights to a leave of absence or the need to offer reasonable accommodation under the disability discrimination laws.

If an employer warns an employee in writing that he or she will be terminated if a course of absenteeism or tardiness persists, that employee may be denied unemployment insurance benefits if the employer can demonstrate that the employee intentionally and continually disregarded warnings to show up for work on time.

Employers should take care that disciplinary action relating to absenteeism is consistent with their obligations under the disability discrimination and state and federal leave laws, where appropriate.

LEAVES OF ABSENCE AND TIME OFF

Employers are encouraged to establish and publish to employees rules governing leaves of absence and time off and to apply those rules on a nondiscriminatory basis. For employers subject to the Family and Medical Leave Act (FMLA), the employer is required by law to publish policies regarding the FMLA. The employer must also post the notice of employee rights under the FMLA at all work locations. The poster may be downloaded from http://www.dol.gov/esa/whd/regs/compliance/posters/fmla.htm.

DISABILITY LEAVE

Some employers provide time off for disability leave but guarantee reinstatement to the employee's same job or to any job only as required by law. Reinstatement, unless otherwise required by law, should depend upon the business needs of the employer. The subject of reinstatement, to which job and at what pay, should be discussed prior to the leave.

Disability leave should be available to employees on at least as favorable a basis as leaves for other purposes, such as unpaid leave for child care. For example, if an employer permitted a female employee to take a four month unpaid leave of absence for child care purposes with full reinstatement to the same job and at the same pay, the employer should provide a disabled employee with at least four months of disability leave, with full reinstatement.

There are many factors which enter into these decisions, such as the company's legitimate business needs and the duty of reasonable accommodation under the discrimination laws. The best protection is for employers to apply their leave policies consistently to individuals of both sexes, all races, ages, etc. and regardless of disability.

Employers should, of course, notify their employees of all short and long term disability benefits. All disability leave policies are subject to the Family and Medical Leave Act requirements, discussed below, for employers subject to that Act.

PERSONAL LEAVE

Personal leave is granted by employers for a variety of reasons, including personal appointments, child care, educational or family responsibilities. The employer should have a published policy which indicates that the grant of personal leave is at the complete discretion of the employer and is available only if the leave will not result in a business hardship for the employer. All personal leaves must be granted on a nondiscriminatory basis. For example, an employer who permits a male employee six months of personal leave for nonwork-related educational purposes should permit six months personal leave to a female employee for a nonmedically-related reason, such as child care, unless the individual workplace situations of the employees are so different that the employer would suffer an undue hardship by treating the employees identically. Personal leave policies are subject to the Family and Medical Leave Act requirements, discussed below, for employers subject to that Act.

FAMILY AND MEDICAL LEAVE

The federal Family and Medical Leave Act ("FMLA") provides eligible employees with the right to take unpaid leave in connection with the birth or adoption of a child, the employee's own serious health condition, the serious health condition of the employee's spouse, child or parent, the serious illness or injury of a covered servicemember, or any qualifying exigency (as discussed further in this section).[300] The discussion which follows is a brief overview of this complex law and its regulations.

Employers should note that the Department of Labor recently released final revised regulations regarding the Family and Medical Leave Act, including regulations that provide additional detail on the FMLA military leave provisions (i.e. leave for a qualifying exigency or to care for a covered servicemember) contained in the National Defense Authorization Act of 2008 ("NDAA") signed into law on January 28, 2008. The new regulations became effective on January 16, 2009. The regulations are available at the Federal Department of Labor's website: dol.gov/esa/whd/fmla/finalrule.htm

The FMLA applies to any employer employing 50 or more employees for 20 or more weeks in the current or prior calendar year. In determining the number of employees, the employer must include its employees on leave of absence or on disciplinary suspension and must include temporary employees on the payroll of another employer.[301] The employer should only count employees on leave or suspension when the employer reasonably suspects they will return to active employment. To be eligible for FMLA leave, an employee: (1) must be employed at a worksite where 50 or more employees are employed by the employer within 75 miles of that worksite; (2) must have been employed by the employer for at least 12 months (the months need not be consecutive); and (3) must have worked at least 1,250 hours in the 12-month period preceding the leave. Employers must keep accurate records of hours worked by their employees in order to establish eligibility or noneligibility of employees' rights to leave under the FMLA.

An eligible employee may take up to 12 weeks of unpaid leave during any 12-month period for the following reasons: (1) in conjunction with the birth or adoption/foster care of a child; (2) for the employee's own "serious health condition"; (3) for the serious health condition of a spouse, parent, or minor or incompetent child; (4) for an eligible employee who is the spouse, child, parent or "next of kin" to care for a covered servicemember (up to 26 weeks); or (5) for a qualifying exigency arising out of the fact that a spouse, child, or parent of an employee is on active military duty, or has been notified of an impending call to active military duty. FMLA may run concurrently with other leave, such as workers' compensation, PTO, vacation, sick leave, etc.

The statute and regulations generally define a "serious health condition" as:

1. any inpatient hospitalization;

2. a period of incapacity of more than 3 days that also involves either

   a. treatment 2 or more times by a health care provider; or

   b. treatment once, with a regimen of continuing treatment.

3. incapacity due to pregnancy (or for prenatal care);

4. chronic conditions requiring treatment;

5. permanent or long-term conditions requiring supervision; or

6. non-chronic conditions requiring multiple treatments.

When there is doubt whether a condition qualifies as "serious" under the FMLA the employer may require the employee to obtain medical certification. Employees must respond to all requests for certification within a 15-day period, unless they are unable to meet the deadline despite diligent, good faith efforts. Employers should not arbitrarily or unilaterally decide whether a claimed medical condition meets the standards established by the FMLA. Medical certification forms are available at the Department of Labor website.

When an employee requests FMLA leave, or when an employer acquires knowledge that an employee's leave may be for an FMLA qualifying reason, the new DOL regulations require the employer to notify the employee of his/her eligibility to take FMLA leave within five business days, absent extenuating circumstances. Similarly, once an employer has obtained sufficient information to determine whether an employee's leave will be protected by the FMLA—such as information obtained from a medical certification—the employer must also notify the employee within five business days that the leave is designated as FMLA leave, absent extenuating circumstances. If the employer has sufficient information, it may provide both the eligibility and designation notices to the employee at the same time. If the employee is eligible for FMLA leave, the new regulations also require that the employee received a written notice of "Rights and Responsibilities" at the time of their eligibility notice detailing the specific expectations and explaining any consequences of the employee's failure to meet such obligations.

Use of FMLA leave should be established with the employee at the commencement of the leave. Leave in conjunction with the birth, adoption or foster care of a child must be taken within one year of the birth, adoption or foster care placement. Leave in connection with a serious health condition may be available on an intermittent or reduced hour basis if medically necessary. For example, an employee may take off several days per month or an hour per day so long as the total reduction is not more than 12 weeks of work per year.

During the leave, the employer must continue to pay the employer's share of the employee's health insurance benefits on the same basis as before the employee went on leave (discussed in the Benefits section of this Guide). Employers may require employees to use any accrued paid vacation, PTO, personal, medical or sick leave as part of the 12-week period, such that the sum of the accrued time off plus FMLA leave does not exceed 12 weeks. Employers should notify employees that other accrued time off will be counted toward the 12-week FMLA period but failure to provide such notice does not entitle the employee to another 12 weeks of leave.[302]

At the end of the leave, an employee must be restored to his or her prior position or to a position with equivalent benefits, pay, and other conditions of employment unless the employee would otherwise have been subject to layoff during the leave. There are exceptions for "key employees," defined as the top ten percent highest paid salaried employees within 75 miles of the workplace. To preserve its right not to reinstate a "key" employee, the employer must notify the employee of the decision not to reinstate prior to the leave.

The NDAA contains important amendments to the FMLA, particularly for military families. The NDAA created two new circumstances in which employees with family members in the armed services may be entitled to FMLA leave.

The NDAA amendments to the FMLA added the following leave entitlements for eligible employees.[303]

First, the FMLA now provides a fifth reason for FMLA leave that permits an eligible employee to take up to 12 weeks of leave in any 12-month period because of a "qualifying exigency" arising out of the fact that a spouse, child, or parent of an employee is on active military duty, or has been notified of an impending call to active military duty.[304] The revised regulations issued by the DOL in late 2008 define "qualifying exigency" by providing a list of reasons for which an eligible employee can take leave under this provision.[305] These reasons are divided into eight general categories: (1) short-notice deployment, (2) military events and related activities, (3) childcare and school activities, (4) financial and legal arrangements, (5) counseling, (6) rest and recuperation, (7) post-deployment activities, and (8) additional activities.[306]

Employees must provide notice of their intent to take active duty leave that is "reasonable and practical."[307] However, because of the "exigent" nature of this type of leave, employers should be prepared to receive only limited notice.

Second, the NDAA amendment adds "Servicemember Family Leave" to the FMLA. Under this provision, an eligible employee who is the spouse, child, parent or "next of kin" of a "covered servicemember" can take up to 26 weeks of leave in a "single 12-month period" to care for the covered servicemember who is recovering from a serious illness or injury sustained in the line of duty.[308] Under the DOL revised regulations, the term "covered servicemember" means a member of the Armed Forces (including the National Guard or Reserves) who is undergoing medical treatment, recuperation, or therapy, is otherwise in outpatient status, or is on the temporary disability retired list, for a serious injury or illness.[309]

As noted in this Guide, the FMLA permits employers to require certification by a health care provider of request for leave relating to a serious health condition. While the amendments allow employers to require certification of requests for leave pertaining to care for a service member's injury,[310] employers are cautioned to ensure that certification forms (including those previously available from the Department of Labor) appropriately address the circumstances and eligibility criteria applicable to the new military leave allowances. New forms are available on the Federal Department of Labor website.

Employers should note that because the NDAA amended the FMLA—and not the Uniformed Services Employment and Reemployment Rights Act ("USERRA")—it applies only to employers with 50 or more employees. As discussed elsewhere, USERRA guarantees leave and protects an eligible employee's job for up to five years for members of the military reserves and national guard who are called away for active duty. Employers should also be mindful of provisions under Minnesota state law requiring employers to grant leave for military families to attend military ceremonies (e.g. a send-off or homecoming ceremony)[311] and as needed when a service member is injured or killed while on active duty.[312]

In light of both the amendments to the FMLA and state law developments, employers are advised to become familiar with the new military family leave options available to employees and take steps to notify employees of the new types of leave. Additionally, employers should also consider revising leave policies—including those set forth in employee handbooks—and forms to reflect these considerable changes. Employers should proceed with caution and consider contacting experienced legal counsel to ensure compliance with military leave laws.

Given the complexities of this law and the confusion which arises when FMLA, disability discrimination and workers' compensation laws all apply to certain situations, employers are also advised to seek the advice of legal counsel to ensure compliance with the FMLA and its various regulations, particularly in light of the recent NDAA amendments and revised regulations issued by the DOL.

PARENTAL LEAVE

Minnesota statutes contain provisions concerning leaves of absence which overlap with the FMLA in certain areas. Employers are required to apply the most generous provision where the laws overlap or conflict. Minnesota employers with 21 or more employees at at least one work site must permit employees who have worked at least half-time for the preceding 12 months to take an unpaid leave of absence of up to six weeks in conjunction with the birth or adoption of a child.[313]

The following rules apply to parental leave:

- The leave must be made available to natural and adoptive fathers and mothers who have been employed for at least one year and who work an average of at least half time per week.

- The six weeks of leave may be reduced by any period of paid parental or disability leave already provided by the employer, so that total leave does not exceed six weeks. Unlike leave under the FMLA, the six weeks of parental leave may not be reduced by accrued sick days to which the employee is entitled, unless the employee agrees.

- The employer may adopt policies governing the timing of requests for unpaid leave. The employee has the right to determine the timing of the leave, except that the leave must begin no later than six weeks after the birth or adoption.

- The employee may continue all group insurance during the leave at his or her own expense.

- The employee must be permitted to return to his or her former position or to a comparable position at the same rate of pay, except if the employee would have otherwise been subject to layoff during the leave. The employee retains all accrued pre-leave benefits and seniority.

- If the leave is longer than one month, the employee must give the employer at least two weeks' notice prior to returning to work.

SICK CHILD CARE LEAVE

Minnesota employers with more than 21 employees at at least one work site must allow employees to use accrued personal sick leave benefits for absences due to illness of their children, for reasonable periods of time, on the same terms as the employees are able to use sick leave benefits for their own illnesses.[314] The child must be under age 18 or under age 20 if he or she is attending secondary school. To qualify for sick child care leave, an employee must have worked for the employer on at least a half time basis for the preceding 12 months.

BONE MARROW LEAVE

Minnesota employers with 20 or more employees at at least one work site must grant a paid leave of absence of up to 40 work hours to an employee who seeks to undergo a medical procedure to donate bone marrow.[315] The employer may not retaliate against the employee for requesting or obtaining the leave. The employer may require a doctor's statement verifying the purpose and length of the leave. If there is a medical determination that the employee does not qualify as a bone marrow donor, paid leave granted prior to the medical determination is not forfeited. There is no requirement that the employee be employed by the employer for a certain period of time before becoming eligible for the leave.

SCHOOL LEAVE

Minnesota employers with one or more employees at at least one work site must grant unpaid leave of up to a total of 16 hours during any 12-month period to enable a parent to attend the special education, pre-school or school conferences or school-related activities of their children or foster children if those conferences or activities cannot be scheduled during nonwork hours.[316] While employees need not be paid for school leave, they may use accrued paid vacation leave or other appropriate leave for this purpose. Where the need for school leave is foreseeable, the employee must give the employer reasonable prior notice and must make a reasonable effort to schedule the leave so as not to unduly disrupt operations.

VACATION

Minnesota employers are not required by law to provide vacation time for their employees; however, paid vacation is almost universally provided to employees. Employers should notify employees how vacation days accrue, whether vacation days can be carried over from year to year, or whether vacation is forfeited if unused at the end of the year. Employers should also tell their employees whether they will be paid for unused accrued vacation time at termination of employment. Although such payment is not necessarily required by Minnesota law (i.e., "use it or lose it" policies are permitted), most employers do pay for unused accrued vacation time at termination.

Minnesota employers have encountered considerable confusion regarding the issue of whether accrued, but unused vacation and paid time off ("PTO") must be paid to an employee at the end of employment. The Minnesota Supreme Court recently cleared up this confusion, finding that employers may impose conditions on payments for unused vacation or PTO upon termination of employment when the conditions are incorporated into a clear policy.[317] More specifically, the court stated that although vacation and PTO benefits are "wages" under applicable Minnesota law, employers may legally adopt and enforce a written policy to not pay earned, but unused vacation or PTO benefits to a departing employee who failed to provide the required notice for his or her resignation or was terminated for misconduct (as was the situation before the court).[318] The court also commented with approval on employers' written policies relating to capping the amount of accrued vacation or PTO benefits and "use-it-or-lose-it" vacation or PTO benefits— both of which are common practices among employers.

In light of the forgoing, employers should review their current vacation and PTO policies to ensure that the policies clearly communicate the employer's intended policy choices. Finally, if an employer decides to change these policies, it is imperative to communicate the new policies to employees—including securing a proper acknowledgment. Policies that directly establish what, if anything, is owed at the time of termination and under what conditions must simultaneously preserve the employment-at-will status of each employee.

If the employer has a vacation policy stating that employees will be paid any unused, accrued vacation at termination, failure to make such payments may result in an employer being found guilty of a gross misdemeanor.[319]

HOLIDAYS

Most Minnesota employers provide paid holidays to their full time employees for New Year's Day, Memorial Day, Independence Day, Labor Day, Thanksgiving and Christmas. In addition, some employers may include Martin Luther King's birthday (third Monday in January), Presidents' Day (third Monday in February), Good Friday, the day after Thanksgiving and part or all of Christmas Eve Day and New Year's Eve Day. Some employers also provide paid time off for an employee's birthday or "personal" days. The law does not require that employees be paid for holidays, nor that employees who work on holidays be paid at a premium rate.

Holiday, vacation and sick days need not be counted as time worked for purposes of the wage and hour laws.

COMPARISON OF FEDERAL AND MINNESOTA FAMILY/MEDICAL/PARENTAL LEAVE LAWS

	MINNESOTA LAW	FEDERAL LAW
Covered Employer	An employer employing 21 or more employees at a single work site.	An employer employing 50 or more employees.
Eligible Employee	An individual who has worked for at least one year for the employer and worked at least half time in the 12-month period preceding the leave.	An individual who is employed at a worksite where 50 or more employees are employed by the employer within 75 miles of that worksite, has worked for the employer for at least one year and worked at least 1,250 hours in the 12-month period preceding the leave.
When Leave Can Be Taken	In conjunction with (a) the birth or adoption of a child (parental leave); or (b) the illness or injury of a child, where the employee's attendance with the child is necessary and consistent with the employer's sick leave policy for employees (sick child care leave). Paid sick child care leave is required only if paid from the employer's general assets. An employee working at least 20 hours a week may also receive paid leave of up to 40 hours to donate bone marrow.	In conjunction with (a) the birth or adoption of a child; (b) the employee's own serious health condition; (c) the serious health condition of a spouse, parent, or minor or incompetent child; (d) the serious illness or injury of a covered servicemember; or (e) any qualifying exigency.
Length of Leave	For parental leave, up to 6 weeks, to commence not later than 6 weeks after birth or adoption. For sick child care leave, for reasonable periods as the employee's attendance with the child is necessary, consistent with the employer's policy for employee sick leave.	For the serious illness or injury of a covered servicemember, up to a total of 26 weeks per year. For all other leave, up to a total of 12 weeks per year. In the case of adoption or birth of a child, leave must be taken within 12 months of the birth or placement. In the case of a leave due to a serious health condition, the leave may be available on an intermittent or reduced hour basis.

Paid or Unpaid Leave	Parental leave may be unpaid. However, paid parental or disability leave, except for accrued sick days, may be considered part of the 6-week parental leave period.	An employer may require the employee to use accrued paid vacation, personal, medical or sick leave as part of the 12-week leave period.
Insurance Benefits	The employee may continue coverage under the employer's group insurance policies during leave at the employee's own expense.	The employer must pay its normal portion of the employer's group health insurance premium during the leave period. The employee may be required to pay the employee portion.
Return to Work	Employees on parental leave must be returned to their former or comparable positions, except where the employee would otherwise have been laid off during the leave. Employees taking sick child care leave must be returned to their former positions.	Employees must be returned to their former or equivalent positions, except if the employee would otherwise have been laid off during the leave. There are certain exceptions for the highest paid 10 percent of the employer's employees.
Notices Required of Employers	Posting of Minnesota leave rights by employers is optional. A brochure can be requested by calling the Minnesota Department of Labor and Industry at (651) 284-5042 or on the Internet at www.doli.state.mn.us/posters.html.	Employers subject to the Act are required to display a poster prepared by the federal Wage and Hour Division (obtainable by calling (612) 370-3371 or on the Internet at www.dol.gov/esa/whd/regs/compliance/posters/fmla.htm). Employers have extensive notification requirements in addition to the poster.
Notices Required of Employees	Employers may require reasonable employee notice of parental leave. Employees must provide two weeks advance notice of return from parental leave if the leave is longer than one month. An employee seeking sick child care leave must provide the same notice required as for sick leave for that employee.	Employees are to give 30 days notice, or as much notice as practicable. For leave due to a serious health condition, employees are required to make reasonable efforts to schedule treatment so that employer operations are not unduly disrupted.

SICK TIME

Many employers permit employees to accrue a certain number of sick days per year. The employer is advised to publish this policy and also to indicate whether sick days may be carried over from year to year or whether they are forfeited if unused at the end of the year. In addition, the employer should clearly indicate that there will be no pay for unused sick days at termination of employment, if that is the employer's policy.

In some workplaces, it is a hardship for the employer to have employees out sick, particularly where the employee is not really sick but merely wants to use up his or her sick days before the end of the year. To avoid that problem, some employers pay employees for all or a portion of unused sick days at the end of each calendar year. This policy generally reduces absenteeism and the resulting inconvenience to the employer. Other employers simply notify their employees that they may take a reasonable amount of time off if they are sick, as needed, but if the amount of sick time taken becomes excessive, the employer has the right to take disciplinary action for excessive absenteeism regardless of the reason. Since employers with more than 20 employees must permit employees to use their sick time to care for sick children, the employer should consider whether such an open-ended sick leave policy will be abused and cause hardship to the business.

Some employers offer PTO (Paid Time Off) plans that specify a maximum number of days for which the employee will be paid, regardless of the reason (whether for vacation, sick leave, or personal time off).

MILITARY LEAVE

Employers must allow regular employees who are members of the uniformed services (Armed Forces and the Army National Guard and Air National Guard) unpaid time off for military duty and training.[320] In addition, such employees must be reinstated to a position of "like seniority, status and pay" following discharge or release from active duty if:

- The employee's position was not temporary;

- The employee left his or her position to go on active duty or inactive duty training;

- The employee's cumulative length of absence and of all previous absences from a position of employment with that employer did not exceed five years (unless the length of absence exceeds five years because the employee was ordered to remain on duty past the five years or the initial period of obligated service goes beyond five years);

- The employee was discharged or released from active duty under honorable conditions;

- The employee applied for re-employment within 90 calendar days after separation from active duty (subject to certain exceptions if the leave was for a short period) or from hospitalization continuing after such a release for not more than two years; and

- The employee is still qualified to perform the duties of the position.

If the employee is not qualified to perform the duties of his or her former position because he or she became disabled during active duty, but the employee is qualified to perform any other position, the employer must offer the employee the position which he or she can perform.

Reinstated employees are entitled to be reemployed in such a manner as to give them the status they would have enjoyed had they continued their employment during their active duty leave. Thus, for example, they must be reemployed without a loss of seniority. They also are entitled to participate in insurance or other benefits in the same manner as other employees returning from leaves of absence. The employee can also request and use any vacation, annual or similar leave with pay that the employee accrued before the commencement of his or her service. In addition, they cannot be discharged from their position without cause within one year of reinstatement if they served more than 180 days. (If they served more than 30 but fewer than 181 days, they cannot be discharged without cause within 180 days of reinstatement.)

Federal and state laws also prohibit employers from refusing to hire individuals or discharging employees based on their membership in the Reserves or National Guard, or from denying such employees a promotion or any other advantage of employment on that basis.

Employers may request that an employee take a proposed military leave for training purposes at a different time. However, an employer may neither require that a leave be rescheduled, nor discipline or discharge an employee who takes a leave notwithstanding a request to reschedule it. Reservists or National Guard members who are called to active duty are not required to notify their employers before the leave commences, and may even be prohibited for security reasons from doing so. There is no annual limit on the amount of training or duty in which the Reserves or National Guard may ask their members to participate.

Upon being informed that an employee will be taking time off for military duty or training, an employer may wish to verify the employee's assignment. A reservist or National Guard member should be able to provide his or her employer with the names and telephone numbers of military personnel who can verify the leave and the date on which the employee received notice of the assignment. Employer Support for the Guard and Reserve, a civilian organization affiliated with the military, can answer employers' questions regarding military leave and their obligations under federal law. Call (800) 336-4590 (or www.esgr.com).

Also, active duty members of the military (including reservists and National Guard members in active service) may suspend or defer certain legal obligations while in service.

First, active duty military personnel are effectively shielded from certain court actions, such as civil suits, bankruptcy, foreclosure and dissolution of marriage while in active service. Lawsuits can be stayed or postponed at any stage of the proceedings. This is not indefinite, and the burden is on the defendant to show that his or her military service affects his or her ability to appear in court or properly answer the charges. If a default judgment is entered against a party who failed to defend against a claim because of military service, he or she may reopen the judgment by application to the court within limited time periods following completion of active duty.

Second, military members are permitted to "cap" interest rates on credit card debt, mortgages and certain other loans through the duration of active duty. A military member must apply to the lender for the interest rate "cap" and must meet certain conditions to qualify. A military member may also obtain temporary relief from mortgage payments if military service materially affects his or her ability to make the mortgage payments.

Third, military members entering active service may lawfully terminate residential and commercial leases. Members or their dependents may be temporarily protected from eviction if their ability to pay rent is materially affected by military service. Landlords may be subject to fines and criminal sanctions if they evict a protected military member.

Several other protections exist for members of the military service which are not enumerated here, including tax relief and abatement and voting rights. Military members called to active duty should review their rights and protections. Employers are advised to contact legal counsel to discuss their obligations with respect to employees on military leave.

JURY DUTY

An employer must permit employees to report for jury duty or to respond to a summons without any adverse employment action or threats against the employee.[321] An employer who violates this rule may be fined up to $700, imprisoned for up to six months, required to reinstate the employee, required to pay damages for lost wages for up to six weeks and required to pay reasonable attorneys' fees.

Many employers have policies which provide employees with the difference between their normal wages and the wages they receive as jurors. If the employer has such a policy, it may want to consider limiting the time period during which the supplemental wages will be provided, for example, for a two-week period.

VOTING TIME

Minnesota employees are entitled to take time off work without loss of pay to vote in a regularly scheduled state primary or general election, an election to fill the vacancy in the office of United States Senator, United States Representative, State Senator or State Representative, or a presidential primary.[322] That right is only available to the employee during the morning of the election. An employer's violation of the law is a criminal misdemeanor.

An employer must also provide an individual with paid time off to serve as an election judge, provided the individual gives the employer at least 20 days' advance written notice.[323] The employer may reduce the employee's pay by the amount the employee is paid to serve as an election judge.

MEAL AND BREAK TIMES

Minnesota employers must provide an employee time to eat a meal when that employee works eight or more consecutive hours.[324] An employer is not required to pay the employee for the meal break unless it is for fewer than 20 minutes or the employee is not completely relieved of his or her duties.

Under Minnesota law, an employer also must allow each employee adequate time to use the restroom once during each four consecutive hour period of work.[325]

An employer is also required under Minnesota law to provide a reasonable break time each day for a nursing mother who needs to express breast milk for her infant child. The break time should run concurrently with any break time already provided to the employee. The employer must also make reasonable efforts to provide a room or other location other than a restroom where the employee can express her milk in privacy.[326]

EMPLOYEE ACCESS TO PERSONNEL FILES

All Minnesota employers are required to provide employees with access to their personnel records.[327]

Minnesota law requires that employers with at least 20 employees must provide written notice to a job applicant upon hire of the rights and remedies provided in Minnesota's statutes governing personnel records.[328] Aside from requiring written notice, the law does not detail either the method by which notice must be given or the specific contents of the required notice. However, an employer might logically elect to provide notice through its employee handbook, along with prominently posting the notice at the workplace. As with any required notice, it is imperative to secure a signed acknowledgment from each employee documenting the required notice.

"Employee" includes former employees who have been separated from employment for less than one year. The procedure with respect to employee access to personnel files is as follows:

- If the employee serves a written request upon the employer to review his or her personnel record, the employer must permit a review of the original personnel file or an accurate copy within seven working days of receiving the request (14 working days if the file is located outside Minnesota).

- The file (or a copy) must be available for review during the employer's normal working hours at or near the workplace.

- The employer need not make the file available to an employee during his or her working hours.

- The employer may have someone present to monitor the review.

- An employee is entitled to review his or her record only once every six months. A former employee may review his or her personnel file once each year after separation for as long as the personnel record is maintained.

- The content of the personnel file which is available to employees is specifically defined in the statute and excludes many items, including, for example, statements of co-workers relating to an employee's alleged misconduct. Legal counsel should be consulted before review of any personnel file which could contain controversial material.

- After reviewing the employment file, the employee may obtain a copy of the file, upon written request to the employer. Former employees may make a written request for, and are entitled to receive, a copy of the file without first reviewing the file. Employers are not permitted to charge employees for copying their files.

- If, after receiving the requested materials, the employee disagrees with specific information in the personnel file, the employee may ask the employer to remove the information. Such request need not be in writing.

- If the employer refuses to remove or revise the disputed material, the employee can submit a written response to the disputed information not to exceed five pages. Such response must be included with the disputed information and must be provided to any other party receiving the disputed information.

- If an employer complies with these procedures, the employer may not be the subject of a lawsuit for defamation, libel or slander based on information contained in the personnel record which is communicated by the employee after review of his or her file.

- The protection afforded by this statute is limited and does not mean that an employer is free to disseminate any portion of any employee's personnel file. In fact, the employer should not reveal the contents of any employee's personnel file unless required to do so by law or under compelling circumstances and only after consultation with legal counsel.

- Employees are protected from retaliation for asserting their rights under this law.

ACCESS TO EMPLOYEE ASSISTANCE RECORDS

Upon written request by a person who received assistance under an employee assistance plan (or the parent or legal guardian of a minor who received assistance), an employee assistance provider must provide an opportunity to review and make copies of the employee assistance records.[329] The time period for complying with such a request is the same as the time for responding to a request to review a personnel file. No copying charge may be assessed.

Employee assistance records must be kept separately from personnel records and must not become part of the employee's personnel file.[330] No portion of the employee assistance records may be disclosed to a third party (including the employer) without prior authorization from the person receiving services or their legal representative.[331] The only exceptions to the nondisclosure rule are disclosures pursuant to state or federal law or a court order, disclosures required in the normal course of providing the employee assistance services, and disclosures to prevent physical harm or the commission of a crime.

PERSONNEL RECORD RETENTION

IN GENERAL

Various statutes require employers to retain employee records for specific time periods. In addition, it is normally in the employer's best interests to retain records through various statute of limitation periods so that the employer can defend itself against various employment law claims.

An exhaustive list and analysis of these requirements is beyond the scope of this Guide. The safest course would be to retain all records indefinitely. For example, a dispute involving pension benefit eligibility could necessitate a review of 20 years of wage and hour records.

For employers who wish to adopt a voluntary record destruction program, some general guidelines are as follows:

- Retain all records relating to benefits and benefit determinations for at least six years beyond final payment under the particular benefit program.

- Any materials relating to possible discrimination claims, including performance reviews and disciplinary comments, should be kept for a minimum of three years.

- Any contractual documents should be kept for at least two years following the final termination date of the contract.

MEDICAL RECORDS

All medical records and medical information obtained from or regarding applicants and employees must be collected and maintained on separate forms and in separate medical files, to be treated as confidential medical records. However, the employer may inform supervisors and managers of required employee work restrictions and necessary accommodations; first aid personnel may be informed if emergency treatment of an employee may be required; and government officials may be provided relevant information, for purposes mandated by law.

PRIVACY

Minnesota law permits employees to sue their employers for invasion of privacy in three situations: (1) intrusion into seclusion (i.e. personal and private matters); (2) publication of personal information that others do not need to know and that employees reasonably expect to remain private; and (3) misappropriation of someone's name, picture, or likeness without their consent.[332] The exact scope of claims for invasion of privacy is not clear, but probing into employees' personal lives and sharing information that employees might expect to remain confidential may pose some potential problems. Also, employers should exercise care when making employment decisions based upon an employee's lifestyle or off-duty conduct. Minnesota law provides certain protections in these situations and employers should consider that employees may expect privacy under some circumstances.

One rapidly developing area of the law concerning privacy issues is the use of computers, electronic mail, voice mail, and other electronic communication systems. Employers may have legitimate reasons to monitor these systems, such as investigating theft or disloyalty, avoiding conflicts of interest, and disciplining employees who engage in misconduct. However, employers should also be aware that these communication systems might contain information that employees expect to keep private – anything from grocery lists typed on the computer to romantic messages exchanged on voice mail or e-mail.

Both the Electronic Communications Privacy Act of 1986 and the Minnesota Privacy Act impose certain criminal and civil penalties on anyone who intentionally intercepts electronic communications between the sender and recipient.[333] Absent some exceptions, these statutes seemingly prohibit employers from monitoring or retrieving information on various electronic communications systems. However, these statutes contain two major exceptions that permit employers to monitor certain communications:

(1) Electronic communications may be monitored when one or both of the parties to the communication consents to the monitoring. For example, if an employee signs an acknowledgment to an employee handbook that contains a policy permitting the employer to monitor its computers, telephones, and other means of electronic communication, the employee has given actual consent to such monitoring. Consent may also be implied. Thus, if an employer clearly explains to its employees that it may monitor computers, telephones, and other electronic communication devices and if the employee continues to use them, the employee has given implied consent to the interception. Note that the employer may review work-related and personal communications regardless of subject matter if the employee gives consent.

(2) A "business use" exception permits the provider of electronic communication systems to monitor them in the ordinary course of business. For example, telecommunications companies may review telephone calls on their equipment and any company providing computers and e-mail to its workforce may review the materials on its equipment so long as the review is in the ordinary course of business. Because this exception is narrower than the consent exception discussed above, care should be used not to monitor communications that are unrelated to the business.

The following are suggestions for dealing with the privacy issues arising from the monitoring of electronic communications:

- **Establish policies.** Inform current and potential employees in writing that various electronic communication systems available to them should be used only for business purposes and that use for improper purposes including, for example, harassment or pornography, is prohibited. Also inform them that the systems may be monitored from time to time and that discipline may be imposed upon employees who are using the systems inappropriately. Obtain consent to monitoring by requiring employees to acknowledge receipt of the policy itself or an employee handbook containing the policy.

- **Follow the policies**. Periodically check the electronic information in the workplace to make sure that employees are not sending sexually harassing messages, misappropriating confidential information, or otherwise abusing the system. Monitor in a nondiscriminatory way regardless of an employee's race, gender, national origin, or membership in some other protected class.

- **Limit monitoring as much as possible**. Even if the employee has given some type of consent, limit monitoring to avoid employee fears that "Big Brother" is always watching or listening. If the monitoring suggests the employee has abused the electronic communications system, gather enough evidence to prove the abuse but then stop. If the employee is sending personal messages despite a policy to limit use of computers to work-related reasons, obtaining one or two personal messages is enough. It is not necessary to monitor all personal messages. Likewise, if an employer acts under the "business use" exception, interception should be limited to business matters. If interception shows that an employee is diverting away business opportunities, gather evidence of the diversion but do not use the interception to monitor that employee's purely personal affairs.

- **Limit disclosure of acquired information to people with a need to know.** Do not make intercepted information available to anyone other than the persons who regularly deal with discipline and termination issues. Train these persons that intercepted information may be highly personal, confidential, embarrassing, and the basis for a defamation claim if the information is false and is communicated to others.

In addition to these policies, remind employees that messages sent on electronic systems may survive even though the sender believes they have been discarded. Courts are permitting discovery of archived computer messages and other communications that are retrievable long after the sender thought they were deleted from the system. Sensitive employment matters should be discussed one-on-one, in the privacy of an office or other appropriate location, rather than on voice mail or e-mail.

Finally, because employee privacy is a rapidly changing area of the law, and Congress has debated various bills that would restrict an employer's ability to monitor electronic communications, consultation with legal counsel is highly recommended to determine the state of the law at any given time.

SHAREHOLDER-EMPLOYEES AND OTHER OWNER EMPLOYEES

Many businesses in Minnesota are organized as non-public or "private" corporations. Private corporations are those whose shares are not regularly traded on a recognized public market.

The issue of who owns shares in a private corporation is important, not only in terms of equity ownership and voting control, but with respect to the rights and liabilities to and among the shareholders, officers, directors and employees in such corporations. The same is true for members, governors and managers in limited liability companies (LLCs) and for partners in Minnesota partnerships.

THE RIGHTS AND DUTIES AMONG SHAREHOLDERS, OFFICERS AND DIRECTORS IN PRIVATE CORPORATIONS

The law controlling companies incorporated in Minnesota generally holds that shareholders, officers and directors owe duties of good faith and loyalty to each other and to the corporation.[334] Frequently, these duties are described as being "fiduciary" in nature. In making decisions regarding the conduct of business matters, it is therefore important for the controlling officers, directors and shareholders to evaluate, on a case-by-case basis, whether their chosen course of action may violate any of their duties to the shareholders or to the corporation. The courts have defined these duties as follows:

- **Director's and Officer's Duty**. A director or officer has the general duty to act in good faith, in a manner reasonably believed to be in the best interests of the corporation and its shareholders, with the care an ordinarily prudent person in a like position would exercise under similar circumstances and to avoid acts of self-dealing and conflicts of interest.

- **Shareholder's Duty**. The controlling shareholder(s) in every private corporation has a duty to the minority shareholder(s) not to use his control for the purpose of self-dealing, including the conduct of actions which are fraudulent, illegal or unfairly prejudicial to the minority shareholder. All shareholders in closely-held corporations (i.e., those with 35 or fewer shareholders) have a duty to act toward one another and the corporation in good faith, which the courts in Minnesota and elsewhere have defined in terms of varying degrees of fiduciary duty.

In actual practice, the above-described duties are often alleged to have been breached when controlling shareholders, officers or directors act to their personal benefit and/or to the personal detriment of the minority shareholder or the corporation. While there is no complete listing of the circumstances in which these duties are found to have been breached, these claims usually involve such financial and corporate control issues as diverting business opportunities; using funds or services for personal financial gain; withdrawing excess compensation and/or other personally valuable benefits from the corporation; and excluding minority shareholders from the reasonable benefits of ownership in the corporation. Although some of these claims may technically belong to the company, in certain circumstances minority shareholders have asserted these types of claims directly against the majority shareholders, especially where the minority owner can establish some unique injury or damage to his or her investment.

Careful advance and ongoing planning can minimize the risk of breaching these duties.

THE EMPLOYEE AS SHAREHOLDER

Frequently, corporate management is presented with the question of whether to issue shares to key employees either as non-cash incentive compensation or pursuant to a buy-in formula. This type of benefit is attractive because it can be used to attract or retain qualified personnel and increase productivity by granting the employee a proprietary interest in the business. The issuance of shares to an employee, however, raises significant corporate governance and employment law issues which must be considered carefully. Some of the major issues are identified below.

- **Impact on the Employment Relationship**. An employee's ownership of shares can potentially affect the corporation's ability to alter the terms of his or her employment, including the right to terminate the employee's employment. In Minnesota, a court has broad discretion to issue relief to a shareholder who has been improperly harmed in his or her capacity as a shareholder or as an employee. Accordingly, even if employed as a non-contract, "at-will" employee, an employee-shareholder may argue that a termination of his or her employment violated a "reasonable expectation" of continued employment, or other related employment terms, growing out of his or her status as a shareholder. Even though employee-shareholders may not be able to prove the existence of an employment contract, they might nevertheless be able to bring a successful case arising out of the termination of their employment based upon their reasonable expectations of continuing employment.[335] The potential damages in a shareholder case are very large, and may include wages until expected retirement age, dividends and other distributions of corporate profits, the value of stock options that the shareholder was not allowed to exercise, and other missed opportunities to participate in the financial rewards of a company.

  Whether an employee's status as a shareholder creates a reasonable expectation of continuing employment turns upon the unique facts of each case. Among the potentially relevant factors are the amount of money the individual has invested into the company, the level of financial risk undertaken by the employee-shareholder, the degree of effort he or she has spent in making the company successful, discussions among the shareholders about their employment expectations, the policies or practices with respect to other employee-shareholders' desire to manage the company effectively with the minority shareholders' desire to continue employment. Accordingly, careful consideration must be given in both issuing stock to an employee and in modifying such an employee-shareholder's employment terms, including termination of employment. These risks can be minimized by entering into definitive agreements with the employee regarding his or her shareholder rights, as discussed below.

- **Voting Control.** The issuance of additional shares to an employee could impact the voting control over the management of the corporation through the election of directors and selection of officers. Whether the issuance of shares will cause an unacceptable dilution or transfer of voting control should always be evaluated in advance of making any commitment to transfer shares.

- **Disclosure of Corporate Information.** Shareholders in Minnesota corporations generally have the right, without a showing of need, to access certain corporate information that employers may not normally share with all of their employees, including annual financial statements, board resolutions and actions, bylaws, articles and shareholder records. Additionally, upon a showing of proper purpose, shareholders in a privately-held company generally have the right to examine other corporate records.[336] The confidentiality of corporate records should be considered when determining whether to make stock ownership available to employees.

- **Conditions of the Employee's Stock Ownership.** Management should carefully consider the following issues before issuing stock to an employee:

  - What terms will govern the employee's ownership and voting of the stock while employed by the company?

  - Will the employee be allowed to continue to own the shares if employment is terminated?

  - How will the shares be valued and purchased if the employee desires, or is required, to sell them by specific agreement with the corporation?

These questions can be resolved through definitive "shareholder control" and "buy-sell" agreements entered into with the employee in advance of transferring any shares. Under Minnesota law, there is a presumption that such agreements reflect the reasonable expectations of the shareholders to the extent that issues are addressed in the documents.[337] In addition, management may prefer to implement other incentive programs, including "phantom" stock plans, which can give the employee a proprietary interest in the performance of the business while avoiding the stock ownership issues identified above.

Shareholder-employee issues are so complex and significant to the long-term success of a business that company owners and management should obtain competent legal advice prior to entering into any agreements to transfer shares to any employee.

THE RIGHTS AND DUTIES AMONG MEMBERS, GOVERNORS AND MANAGERS IN LIMITED LIABILITY COMPANIES AND AMONG PARTNERS IN PARTNERSHIPS

The members, governors and managers of LLCs formed under Minnesota law have essentially the same duties and responsibilities to one another as do the shareholders, directors and officers in privately-held companies and have heightened responsibilities in closely-held LLCs.[338] The same is true for partners in Minnesota partnerships. Employee ownership issues raise the same concerns in LLCs and partnerships as they do in corporations.

WORKERS' COMPENSATION

PURPOSE AND PHILOSOPHY OF THE WORKERS' COMPENSATION SYSTEM

In the absence of a workers' compensation system, an employee injured while working would in most cases have no recourse for the injury except if the employer, its agents or some third party had been negligent. Most work-related injuries would not be compensable because they are not the result of negligence (e.g., back injuries sustained while lifting) or they are caused by the negligence of the injured employee (e.g., an employee driving a forklift off a dock).

The philosophy of the workers' compensation system is to provide benefits to injured employees under all circumstances where the injury relates to the work activity regardless of whether anyone has been negligent. While this places a greater financial burden on the employer, the employer is able to add the cost to the product or service it provides, thereby spreading this cost of doing business among the consuming public. Furthermore, in exchange for providing these benefits, the exposure of the employer is limited by the workers' compensation law. The employer is responsible only for specifically defined benefits such as wage loss, medical expense and permanent injury. Other damage claims such as those for pain and suffering, emotional distress, or loss of consortium are not permitted. With limited exceptions, these workers' compensation benefits become the only responsibility of the employer to its employees for work-related injuries, and the employer is not subject to other claims or lawsuits even if the injuries were caused by the employer's negligence.

EMPLOYERS SUBJECT TO THE MINNESOTA WORKERS' COMPENSATION LAW

All Minnesota employers, with very limited exceptions, are subject to the Minnesota Workers' Compensation Act.[339] The term "employer" means any person who employs another to perform a service for hire, and includes a corporation, partnership, association, group of persons, a state, a county, a town, a city, a school district or a governmental subdivision.[340] With limited exceptions, any such employer who has one or more employees is subject to the workers' compensation law.

Employees include any persons who provide services to another for hire. Any person—no matter their age, duty, or title—may be included as an employee. Voluntary, uncompensated workers also may fall within the definition of an employee. There are some very limited exclusions to the categories of employees covered by the workers' compensation law.[341] The exclusions to coverage, however, are extremely limited, and no exclusion should be assumed without careful review.

INSURING OR SELF-INSURING AGAINST WORKERS' COMPENSATION CLAIMS

Any employer subject to the Minnesota Workers' Compensation Act must obtain workers' compensation insurance coverage through an insurance company authorized to insure for such liability in the State of Minnesota.[342] Certain employers, if they obtain approval from the Division of Insurance, may self-insure against workers' compensation liability, or may establish a group of self-insurers. In order to qualify as a self-insured employer, the employer must meet stringent requirements including proof of substantial financial stability.[343] Any employer who fails to insure or self-insure is subject to penalties[344] and, in addition to the penalties, remains subject to workers' compensation claims or to broader damage claims in a civil damage action.[345] Insurance companies providing workers' compensation insurance in Minnesota are now required to make available to their insured employers a deductible plan whereby the employer pays up to a set amount per claim.[346] The amount of premium to be paid by an employer who selects a policy with a deductible will be reduced.

Employers may work with their insurance agents or brokers to obtain workers' compensation coverage, or they may seek assistance in obtaining coverage by contacting the State of Minnesota Workers' Compensation Division of the Department of Labor and Industry at (651) 284-5005 or by visiting http://www.doli.state.mn.us/workcomp.html.

THE DETERMINATION OF WORKERS' COMPENSATION INSURANCE PREMIUMS

Insurance premiums employers must pay for workers' compensation insurance are determined by various factors including employee class codes, annual employee payrolls, and the employer's loss experience rating. All employees, depending upon the nature of their work, are placed in a class. These classes, in turn, are evaluated and coded by the degree of risk of injury. The annual payroll for each class is then factored in and a premium calculated. Obviously, the greater the payroll, and/or the higher the risk classes, the greater the premium. In addition, the loss experience rating of the employer is periodically analyzed and factored into the premium structure. An employer may benefit by lowered insurance premiums if the employer is successful in maintaining a safe workplace and in working with injured employees to minimize their lost work time.[347]

EMPLOYERS REQUIRED TO POST NOTICE OF EMPLOYEE'S RIGHTS

Employers are required by law to post at conspicuous locations a notice to employees of their rights under the Minnesota Workers' Compensation Act.[348] These notices advise employees of assistance available to them, the operation of the workers' compensation system, and the name and address of the workers' compensation insurance carrier (or the fact that the employer is self-insured, if applicable). Copies of preprinted notices may be obtained from the Minnesota Department of Labor and Industry, Workers' Compensation Division, 443 Lafayette Road N., St. Paul, MN 55155-4307, (651) 284-5030. In Duluth, employers may contact the Division's Office at 5 North 3rd Avenue W., Suite 400, Duluth, MN 55802-1614, (218) 733-7810 or 1-800-365-4584. Outside the Twin Cities area, there is a toll-free number: 1-800-342-5354.

ACTION TO BE TAKEN BY THE EMPLOYER IN CASE
OF AN INJURY TO AN EMPLOYEE

When an employee is injured, the employer has the responsibility of immediately reporting any such injury to its workers' compensation insurance carrier. Preprinted forms entitled "First Report of Injury" for use in reporting injuries may be obtained either from the Department of Labor and Industry, Minnesota Workers' Compensation Division, or from the insurance carrier or the insurance administrator. If death or serious injury occurs during the course of employment, the employer must report the death or injury to both the Department of Labor and Industry and the insurer within 48 hours.[349] It is the responsibility of the employer, not the employee, to complete the First Report of Injury form. This form must then be sent to the insurance company, and the insurance company will in turn send a report to the Department of Labor and Industry within 14 days after the injury. Failure to meet this reporting period may result in a penalty imposed upon the insurance carrier. Note that the employer must also give the employee the "Minnesota Workers' Compensation System Employee Information Sheet" at the time the employee is given a copy of the First Report of Injury Form.

OSHA regulations require that when an employment-related incident results in the death of at least one employee, or the inpatient hospitalization of at least three employees, the death or hospitalization must be reported within eight hours to the Department of Labor and Industry's OSHA office.[350] After normal business hours and on Saturdays, Sundays and holidays, the report must still be made within eight hours, and is to be made by telephoning the federal OSHA office's toll-free telephone number, which is (800) 321-6742. This reporting requirement applies to employment-related incidents that, within 30 days of their occurrence, subsequently result in the death of one employee, or the in-patient hospitalization of at least three employees. Employers that learn about such reportable incidents after they occur must make the required report within eight hours of the time the incident is reported to any agent or employee of the employer.

Reporting an injury to the workers' compensation insurance carrier or to the Commissioner of Labor and Industry does not constitute an admission that the injury was work-related or that it is covered by the workers' compensation law. These are notice and reporting requirements that must be met as soon as the employer is aware of a claimed injury. The employer and its insurance carrier are not, by virtue of this reporting, precluded from contesting the claim.

Employers are also encouraged to promptly notify their insurance carriers so that an appropriate investigation may be immediately conducted. The employer should not only cooperate fully with the insurance carrier, but may also work with the insurance carrier and assist in the investigation.

BENEFITS UNDER THE WORKERS' COMPENSATION LAW FOR AN INJURED EMPLOYEE

Benefits available for a work-related injury are established by statute. These statutes are frequently amended by the legislature and the statutes in effect at the time of injury must be consulted for specifics. General categories of benefits include the following:[351]

- **Medical and Related Services**. The employee is entitled to medical, chiropractic, surgical and hospital treatment, including nursing, medicines, medical and surgical supplies, crutches, apparatus including artificial members, and other reasonable expenses for care and treatment.

- **Temporary Total Disability**. During the period when an employee is recovering from the injury and unable to work, the employee is entitled to two-thirds of his or her weekly wage at the time of injury, subject to a statutory maximum. An injured employee disabled from work and who has a low weekly wage nevertheless is entitled to a minimum set by statute. This temporary total disability benefit is available throughout the period of the employee's inability to return to work, subject to time limitations, and may be terminated 90 days after the employee has reached maximum medical improvement from the injury, or upon the employee's retirement.

- **Temporary Partial Disability**. If the injured employee is able to work in a partially disabled condition but because of the injury is not able to earn the same amount of money that the employee earned at the time of the injury, the employee is entitled to temporary partial disability. Temporary partial disability is measured by two-thirds of the difference between what the employee was earning at the time of the injury and what the employee is able to earn in the partially disabled condition, subject to statutory maximums. Temporary partial disability is limited to 225 weeks of cumulative benefits, and will not be paid after 450 weeks from the date of injury.

- **Permanent Partial Disability**. Upon cessation of temporary total disability, permanent partial disability becomes payable. If the employee has permanent disability, the percentage of this permanent disability is determined by an evaluating doctor through application of disability schedules.[352] The amount of these benefits is statutorily determined based upon the percentage rating of disability.

- **Permanent Total Disability**. Where an injured employee is permanently and totally disabled from substantial gainful employment, the employee is entitled to permanent and total disability. This compensation is paid during the permanent total disability of the injured employee, but is subject to some reduction if the employee receives disability benefits because of the same injury from a governmental disability benefit program, or if the employee receives old age or survivor benefits under the Social Security law. Permanent total disability benefits typically cease at age 67 because of presumed retirement.

- **Dependency Benefits**. In the case of a fatal work-related injury, limited burial expenses are paid. In addition, dependency benefits are paid to persons dependent upon the deceased employee. Compensation for the spouse is paid at the rate of 50 percent of the employee's weekly wage at the time of injury for a period of ten years. These payments are increased depending upon the number of dependent children up to a maximum of two-thirds of the employee's wage at the time of the accident.

- **Refusal to Offer Continued Employment.** The Minnesota Workers' Compensation Act encourages employers to return injured employees to gainful employment. The Act provides that an employer who, without reasonable cause, refuses to offer continued employment to its employee when employment is available within the employee's physical limitations, may be liable in a civil action for up to one year's wages, subject to a maximum of $15,000. This obligation by the employer is not covered by insurance.[353]

For employers who are insured for workers' compensation coverage, the administration of these numerous benefits is handled by the insurance company or by a third-party administrator. Self-insured employers must, of course, administer their own benefits.

INFORMAL RESOLUTION OF DISPUTES

A vast majority of workers' compensation claims are handled quickly and without problems. The claims are investigated by the insurance carrier or third party administrator and, where appropriate, benefits are voluntarily paid.

Where an injury is work-related and the employee is entitled to benefits, benefits will be paid under the law as noted above. Occasionally, disputes arise with respect to discontinuing benefits after a period of time. A system is in place for resolving such disputes by an administrative conference. An administrative conference is intended as an informal meeting attended by the employee and possibly the employee's attorney, by the employer, by the employer's insurance company, and by a representative of the Department of Labor and Industry. An attempt is made to resolve these disputes through such a conference. If a resolution cannot be voluntarily made, the Department will make a decision. This decision can be appealed.[354]

Additionally, a small claims court has been established for the purpose of quickly and inexpensively resolving disputed claims involving $5,000 or less.[355] If both the employee and employer agree, qualifying claims may be submitted for resolution by the small claims court. It is not necessary that the parties be represented by attorneys. The determination is not appealable, and has binding effect for later proceedings.

PROCEDURE FOR RESOLUTION OF DISPUTED CLAIMS AND RIGHTS OF APPEAL

Disputes over claims arise where the employer and its insurer deny that the injury is work-related, or deny that the benefits claimed are justified. Disputes may also arise over efforts to terminate benefits. When such disputes exist, the insurance carrier will retain legal counsel to represent the interest of the employer in the dispute. These disputes, unless settled, will proceed to a hearing before a workers' compensation judge who will hear the evidence and render a formal decision. The evidence submitted to the judge may include the testimony of witnesses, including testimony of doctors through depositions or medical reports, and occasionally testimony of rehabilitation consultants or other experts. After the hearing, the compensation judge will render a formal written opinion. Any party dissatisfied with the decision of the compensation judge may appeal that decision to the Minnesota Workers' Compensation Court of Appeals. Upon such an appeal, the matter is not retried, but rather, the Court of Appeals determines whether or not the compensation judge's decision was clearly erroneous and not supported by substantial evidence. The Court of Appeals may affirm, modify or reverse the decision, or remand the case. Any party dissatisfied with the decision of the Workers' Compensation Court of Appeals may file a Writ of Certiorari to appeal the matter to the Minnesota Supreme Court.

ACTION FOR CIVIL DAMAGES FOR OBSTRUCTING THE EMPLOYEE SEEKING BENEFITS

An employer discharging or threatening to discharge an employee for seeking workers' compensation benefits, or in any manner intentionally obstructing an employee from seeking workers' compensation benefits, may be found liable in a civil action for damages incurred by the employee including any diminution in workers' compensation benefits, and for punitive damages not to exceed three times the amount of compensation benefits to which an employee is entitled.[356]

THE MANAGED CARE PLAN

The treatment to be provided to an employee under the Workers' Compensation Act may be provided in whole or in part under a Managed Care Plan certified by the Department of Labor and Industry.[357] One of the objectives of this provision is medical cost containment. Certain medical groups such as Health Service Plan Corporations, Health Maintenance Organizations, or Preferred Provider Organizations may apply to the Department of Labor and Industry for certification. In order to be certified, these entities must, among other things, agree to provide quality medical services at reduced service costs. The managed care providers also agree to establish a method of dispute resolution to resolve issues such as the rating of disability.

Employers should discuss with their workers' compensation insurance carriers the availability of such plans and the desirability of implementing the Managed Care Plan for their employees.

TRAINING SESSIONS ON WORKERS' COMPENSATION

From time to time the Minnesota Department of Labor and Industry, Workers' Compensation Division, conducts training sessions for employers. Seminars are also sponsored by private business organizations. For more information on workers' compensation training sessions, contact the Minnesota Department of Labor and Industry at (651) 846-1800.

SAFETY, HEALTH AND ENVIRONMENTAL ISSUES IN THE WORKPLACE

MINNESOTA OCCUPATIONAL SAFETY AND AND HEALTH ACT

The Occupational Safety and Health Division of the Minnesota Department of Labor and Industry administers the Minnesota Occupational Safety and Health Act of 1973. The express purpose of this Act is "to assure so far as possible every worker in the State of Minnesota safe and healthful working conditions and to preserve our human resources."[358] The Minnesota Occupational Safety and Health Codes adopt, by reference, the federal Occupational Safety and Health Standards. In addition, Minnesota has adopted some "localized" standards that apply to hazards not covered by the federal OSHA standards.[359] OSHA standards apply to all places of employment in the state with the exception of those under the exclusive jurisdiction of the federal government.[360]

EMPLOYERS RIGHTS AND RESPONSIBILITIES

An employer's rights and responsibilities under the Act include, but are not limited to, the following:

- An employer must furnish to employees conditions of employment that are free from recognized hazards that are causing or are likely to cause death or serious injury.[361]

- Employers are entitled to participate in the development, revision or revocation of OSHA standards by commenting on proposed standards, participating in hearings concerning standards, or by requesting the development of a new standard.[362]

- An employer may request a variance from the requirements of a particular OSHA standard if the employer is unable to meet the mandates of that standard and wishes to use alternative means of compliance.[363]

- Employers are entitled to protection of trade secrets or other legally privileged communications.[364]

- Employers must post the Occupational Safety and Health Protection on the Job poster in their places of employment.[365] Posters may be obtained by contacting the Minnesota Department of Labor and Industry, 443 Lafayette Road North, St. Paul, MN 55155, (651) 284-5042 (or at www.doli.state.mn.us).

- Employers must provide to their employees free of charge all necessary protective equipment required by OSHA standards.[366]

RECORDKEEPING

Employers must maintain a log of injuries and illnesses prescribed in the Minnesota OSHA Codes and must post an annual summary of those injuries. The OSHA 300 Form (effective January 1, 2004), which is used for this purpose, includes information and instructions for completing the form and is available by contacting the Minnesota Department of Labor and Industry at (651) 284-5042 or visiting www.doli.state.mn.us/recordkeeping.html. This injury and illness information must also be made available to an OSHA investigator should an inspection be conducted at the place of employment.[367]

PENALTIES

Under Minnesota law, an employer who receives a citation for a serious violation of its duties under the Minnesota OSHA standards may be assessed a fine of up to $7,000. If a serious violation of the Minnesota OSHA standards occurs which causes or contributes to the death of an employee, the employer may be assessed a fine of up to $25,000.[368] Minnesota OSHA regulations contain an exception for small employers with fewer than 50 employees: if a violation is not willful or repeated, small employers may be assessed an initial fine of $5,000, and $5,000 for each of the following four years. Minnesota OSHA regulations also provide for criminal penalties of up to $70,000 for a first violation and $100,000 for a subsequent violation.

ERGONOMICS

To date, Minnesota has not promulgated rules with respect to ergonomics. In 2002, however, the Minnesota Department of Labor and Industry (DOLI) established an Ergonomics Task Force to recommend approaches that DOLI can take to reduce work-related musculoskeletal disorders in Minnesota. The task force's final report summarizes all of the ergonomic recommendations made by the members and reviews the work of the task-force. The task-force final report can be reviewed at http://www.doli.state.mn.us/ergo.html.

There are no federal OSHA ergonomic rules in final form. However, the federal OSHA has issued, and will continue to issue, industry-specific guidelines to reduce injuries and illnesses related to musculoskeletal disorders. These guidelines are tools an employer can use to recognize and control hazards. The guidelines are voluntary and, accordingly, employers who fail to implement guidelines that OSHA develops are not in violation of OSHA. Currently, guidelines are available for the shipyards, poultry processing, nursing home and retail grocery store industries. These guidelines can be found at www.osha.gov/SLTC/ergonomics/guidelines.html. Employers in other industries for which guidelines have not been developed may find useful information in these guidelines for developing their own ergonomic programs.

EMPLOYEE RIGHTS AND RESPONSIBILITIES

Although the sole responsibility for compliance with the law rests with the employer, employees are obliged to comply with OSHA standards and regulations which are applicable to their own actions and conduct. Employees cannot be cited or fined for noncompliance; employers must set up their own disciplinary procedures for employees who violate standards or regulations. Employee rights include, but are not limited to, the following:

- Employees have the right to request an OSHA inspection by filing a written complaint with the Minnesota Occupational Safety and Health Division describing the hazardous conditions that exist at the work facility.[369] The complaint must be filed by a current employee and must be signed. A complainant's name is not revealed nor is it part of any inspection record made available for review.

- Employees may participate in standards development activities.[370]

- Employees must be notified of a variance request filed by their employer; employees may petition for a hearing on the variance request.[371]

- Employees may participate in the opening and/or closing conference held prior to or during an OSHA inspection; employees who exercise this right must be paid their usual wage.[372]

- Employees may not be discriminated against because they exercised any right afforded them under the Minnesota OSHA Act.[373]

OSHA INSPECTIONS

OSHA authorizes the Minnesota Department of Labor and Industry to conduct inspections and to issue citations and proposed penalties for alleged violations of OSHA. Inspections are generally prompted by fatalities or accidents which may have occurred at the facility, conditions which represent a continuing imminent danger to employees or an employee complaint. Other inspections may occur during routine programmed inspections for high-hazard industries or occupations. Industries targeted for program inspections are selected based on their death, injury and illness incident rates as well as such factors as employee exposure to toxic substances.

The investigator has the authority to take environmental samples and to take photographs related to the purpose of the inspection.[374] The inspector may also privately question the owner or operator of the facility and its employees.[375] The inspector must comply with all employer safety and health rules and practices at the facility being inspected, and the inspections should be conducted to avoid unreasonable disruption of the operations at the facility.

A representative of the employer and a representative authorized by its employees must be given an opportunity to accompany the inspector during the inspection of the workplace.[376] The inspector may consult with employees concerning matters related to OSHA during the inspection.[377] The authorized representative of the employees must also be given an opportunity to participate in any conference or discussion held prior to or during the inspection.[378] The investigator will hold a private conference with either the employee representative or the employer at either party's request.[379] Under OSHA rules, an employee taking part in the inspection is entitled to his regular pay for the time spent in the inspection.[380]

When the inspector arrives at the facility, management should be immediately notified. As part of employee training, employees should be advised as to the proper procedure to notify management in the event an inspector arrives at the facility. If an OSHA inspector does not have a search warrant, the inspector can be denied access to the facility.[381] However, if the inspector is denied access, the inspector may return with a warrant and may be more likely to take a closer look at the facility because of the concern that the employer was trying to hide something or had the opportunity to correct a violation during the period of time it took the inspector to get the warrant.

At the beginning of an inspection, the inspector should present his or her credentials, explain the nature and purpose of the inspection and indicate generally the scope of the inspection and the records he or she wishes to review, if any.[382] Inspections are generally conducted during regular working hours.[383] If the inspection was prompted by a complaint, the employer should request a copy of the complaint from the inspector. The employer should also ask for an opening conference prior to the commencement of the inspection.[384] During that time, a manager familiar with OSHA's standards and the facility should meet with the inspector and collect information regarding why the inspection is occurring and what areas the inspector would like to inspect and the types of information he or she will be collecting. At that time, the employer can decide whether or not the employer wants to take duplicate photos and duplicate environmental samples.

At the beginning of an inspection, the employer may identify areas in the facility which might reveal trade secrets.[385] Information obtained in such areas during the inspections shall be labeled "Confidential Trade Secret" and may not be disclosed by OSHA.[386]

During the inspection, employers should always have a representative accompanying the inspector.[387] If at all possible, it is beneficial to have two people accompany the inspector, one showing the inspector the areas of the facility and the other taking notes on the inspection. If the employer decides to take photos, they should be taken from the same vantage point as the OSHA inspector or the employer can request that the OSHA inspector provide copies of the photos to the employer. If samples are taken, the employer can request duplicate samples which would be retained by the employer. It is important to record the sample location and the collection methods.

In the event the inspector decides to review company documents, generally only those documents which are required to be maintained under the law, such as the log and summary of occupational injuries and illnesses and the annual summary, need to be disclosed. In the event the OSHA inspector requests facility accident reports, legal counsel should review such reports before they are released.

At the conclusion of the inspection, the inspector must confer with the employer or the employer's representative and then formally advise the employer of any alleged violations discovered during the inspection.[388]

If there is evidence suggesting a violation of OSHA, the inspector will issue the employer either a citation or a notice of violation.[389] A copy of the citation and a proposed assessment of penalty is also provided to the employee representative.[390] The citation should describe the nature of the alleged violation and refer to the provisions of the Act which have been violated and it will fix a reasonable time or times for the abatement of the alleged violation.[391]

The amount of the penalty will generally be related to its potential to cause harm, the company's history of compliance, the size of the company and the degree of control the employer had over the potential for the violation. The amount of the penalty can generally be negotiated with the inspector by providing mitigating information to the inspector related to the factors which go into the assessment of the penalty amount.[392] The imposition of a penalty and the date by which the violation must be corrected can be appealed through OSHA's administrative procedures.[393] The employer or employee may also contest the determination of a citation and both have a right to a hearing before an administrative law judge.[394]

DISCRIMINATION

No employee may be discharged or in any way discriminated against because of filing a complaint with OSHA or exercising any of his or her rights under OSHA.[395] This protection extends to participation in an inspection or providing information to the OSHA inspector during an employee interview.[396]

In addition, an employee may refuse to work if he or she has a reason to believe that imminent danger of death or harm may result from an alleged violation of OSHA.[397] In this circumstance, the employee may have to accept alternative work until the existence of the alleged violation can be verified.[398]

The remedies for discrimination against an employee include back pay, compensatory damages, reinstatement and attorneys' fees.[399] There is also a private right of action available to the employee against the employer.[400]

EMPLOYEE RIGHT-TO-KNOW ACT

The 1983 Minnesota Legislature passed the "Employee Right-to-Know" Act as part of the Minnesota statutes governing occupational safety and health. The Act is intended to ensure that employees are aware of the dangers associated with hazardous substances, harmful physical agents, or infectious agents (which apply only to hospitals and clinics) that they may be exposed to in their workplaces.[401] The Act requires employers to evaluate their workplaces for the presence of hazardous substances, harmful physical agents, and infectious agents and to provide training to employees concerning those substances or agents to which employees may be exposed.[402] Written information on hazardous substances, harmful physical agents or infectious agents must be readily accessible to employees or their representatives.[403] Labeling requirements for containers of hazardous substances and equipment or work areas that generate harmful physical agents are also included.[404]

The Employee Right-to-Know Act generally applies to all Minnesota employers regardless of size.[405] Special provisions apply to certain technically qualified individuals who meet the criteria defined in the standard; farming operations and waste service employers are regulated by the federal Resource Conservation and Recovery Act.[406]

Employers should conduct an inventory of their workplaces to determine what hazardous substances or harmful physical agents are present and which employees are at risk of exposure. Once the survey is completed, the employer must obtain, and have accessible to employees, written information on those substances or agents. This written information is usually in the form of a material safety data sheet (MSDS) which can be obtained from the manufacturer of the substance. Material safety data sheets will provide the basic information that must be presented in the oral training program.

The Employee Right-to-Know standard is being enforced as part of the Minnesota Occupational Safety and Health program.[407] The standard provides guidelines concerning the type of information that must be included in the training program, how often training must be provided, requirements for documentation and maintenance of training records, and labeling of hazardous substance containers and equipment that generates a harmful physical agent.[408] The standard also includes lists of hazardous substances and harmful physical agents to assist employers in evaluating their workplaces.[409]

A copy of the Employee Right-to-Know Standard, which is included in the Minnesota Department of Labor and Industry Occupational Safety and Health Rules, may be obtained by contacting the Minnesota Bookstore, 660 Olive Street, St. Paul, MN 55155, at (651) 297-3000. An employer's guide to developing an Employee Right-to-Know program is available at www.doli.state.mn.us/rtkgen.html. Questions concerning the Employee Right-to-Know Act may be directed to one of the Occupational Safety and Health Division offices listed under OSHA Area Offices.

SMOKING

In response to the increasing awareness of the health risks posed by second hand smoke, many states, including Minnesota, have passed legislation restricting smoking in public places.[410] The Minnesota Clean Indoor Air Act was passed to protect human health and the environment by prohibiting smoking in certain areas and limiting it in other areas. The Act prohibits smoking in health care facilities, including hospitals, clinics and doctors' offices, and in public schools.[411]

Minnesota's "Freedom to Breathe Act" prohibits smoking in virtually all places of employment.[412] The Act is discussed in detail in the Workplace Issues section entitled "Smoking."

Where employers have failed to limit smoking in the workplace, nonsmoking employees have brought civil suits to force their employers to provide clean-air work environments. An increasing number of employees exposed to smoke in the workplace and afflicted with smoke-associated medical disorders are also suing for unemployment benefits, disability payments, and workers' compensation benefits.

SICK BUILDING SYNDROME

In recent years there has been increasing public awareness of dangers resulting from indoor air pollution. Sources of indoor air pollution include formaldehyde in particle board, plywood, furniture and carpet, benzene in synthetic fibers, plastics and cleaning supplies, mercury and lead in paint, asbestos, dust, pollen and mold. Indoor air pollution problems arise when these materials are present in a building with an inadequate or defective ventilation system.

AIDS

In 1986 OSHA first began considering the problem of assuring a safe workplace for employees whose jobs routinely involve exposure to blood or other body fluids and, thus, potential exposure to HIV. While documented transmission of HIV in the workplace has been relatively rare, OSHA has concluded that the risk of injury is real and has promulgated workplace safety rules. The current OSHA rules require employers to establish an infection control program which conforms with OSHA standards for any employees whose job responsibilities give rise to "reasonably anticipated skin, eye, mucous membrane, or parenteral contact with blood or other potentially infectious materials." Such exposures that are neither reasonably nor routinely expected in the normal course of employment are not covered by the OSHA rules.

OSHA standards do not require patients or other recipients of services provided by an employee to disclose their HIV infection. Pursuant to the OSHA rules, where an employee has suffered a needle stick or cut or a splash to eye, nose or mouth of body fluids, the source person must be informed of the incident and tested for HIV infection, after consent is obtained. If the source person refuses testing or tests positive, the employee must be evaluated clinically as soon as possible. If the employee refuses testing after the incident, no adverse action may be taken against the employee.

Employers may be liable for the discriminatory acts of their employees, such as when an employee refuses to provide services to a person infected with HIV or refuses to work with an HIV infected co-worker. Federal nondiscrimination standards, such as those contained in the Rehabilitation Act and the Americans with Disabilities Act, as well as state and local statutes, prohibit such discrimination. Under applicable OSHA regulations, an employee acting in good faith can refuse to perform his job because of a reasonable fear of death or serious injury, when no reasonable, less drastic alternative is available to the employee. The employer cannot discipline or terminate the employee for the refusal. However, OSHA regulations provide that the employee's apprehension of death or serious bodily injury must be of such a nature that a reasonable person, under similar circumstances, would conclude that there is a real danger of death or serious bodily injury and that there is insufficient time due to the urgency of the situation to eliminate the danger by resorting to regular statutory enforcement channels. Under this standard, an employee who is not afforded adequate protective equipment which meets OSHA standards may refuse to work. Such cases, however, would be limited to employment settings such as health care institutions, where employees routinely come in contact with patients' bodily fluids. In most workplaces, the employee's objection to working with a coworker or customer infected with HIV would not be based on a reasonable apprehension of an actual danger. Employer termination or discipline of an employee refusing to work under those circumstances does not violate OSHA standards.

WORKPLACE ACCIDENT AND INJURY REDUCTION PLANS

The Workplace Accident and Injury Reduction Act (AWAIR) requires employers in certain industries to develop and implement written workplace accident and injury reduction programs to promote safe and healthy working conditions. The Commissioner of Labor and Industry has compiled a list of standard industrial classifications (SICs) of employers who must develop these programs.[413] Covered SICs are based on the industry's safety or workers' compensation record and are updated every two years. The list of covered SICs is published in the State Register. (Note that the State Register is available free online at www.admin.state.mn.us). The list of employers can be based upon either SIC codes or the North American Industry Classification System (NAICS).

A written plan must be developed within six months following the date the employer's SIC is placed on the list.[414] The plan must have clearly stated goals and objectives; describe responsibility for its implementation and management participation; methods used to identify, analyze, and control new or existing hazards, conditions and operations; describe communication to affected employees; and describe investigation of workplace accidents, corrective action, and enforcement of safe work practices.[415] The employer must conduct and document a review of the workplace accident and injury reduction plan at least annually and document how procedures set forth in the plan are met.[416]

ON-SITE CONSULTATION SERVICES

Free assistance is available to help private sector employers in small, high-hazard industries improve their safety record, lower accident and workers' compensation costs, and understand OSHA obligations. This service is state and federally funded and is separate from the OSHA enforcement activity. A request for a consultation will not result in an OSHA inspection. Consultants will help employers recognize hazards, make recommendations for solving problems and suggest other sources of help that may be available. A visit to the workplace by a consultant is scheduled at the employer's request for a mutually agreeable time and is followed by a letter giving the consultant's recommendations. The employer's obligation is to correct any serious hazards noted. For information or assistance, contact: MN OSHA Workplace Safety Consultation, Department of Labor and Industry, 443 Lafayette Road North, St. Paul, MN 55155, (651) 284-5060.

OSHA AREA OFFICES

St. Paul

MNOSHA Compliance
443 Lafayette Road N.
St. Paul, MN 55155-4307
Phone: (651) 284-5050
Fax: (651) 284-5741
Toll-free: 1-800-DIA-DL1 (1-800-342-5354)
E-mail: OSHA.Compliance@state.mn.us

Duluth

MNOSHA Compliance
5 N. Third Ave. W., Suite 402
Duluth, MN 55802-1611
Phone: (218) 733-7830
Fax: (218) 725-7722

Mankato

MNOSHA Compliance
410 Jackson Street, Suite 520
Mankato, MN 56001
Phone: (507) 389-6507
Fax: (507) 389-2746

MNOSHA Workplace Safety Consultation
Minnesota Workplace Safety Consultation can be contacted at:

MNOSHA Workplace Safety Consultation
443 Lafayette Road N.
St. Paul, MN 55155-4307
Phone: (651) 284-5060
Fax: (651) 284-5739
Toll-free: 1-800-DIA-DL1 (1-800-342-5354)
E-mail: OSHA.Consultation@state.mn.us

TERMINATIONS

REDUCTIONS IN FORCE

Employers contemplating a reduction in force ("RIF") or large scale layoff should consult legal counsel. Plant closings, substantial layoffs or relocations of operations are subject to the federal Worker Adjustment and Retraining Notification (WARN) Act.[417] In addition, Minnesota employers must report to the Minnesota Commissioner of Employment and Economic Development names, addresses and occupations of employees affected by a plant closing, substantial layoff or relocation of operations.[418] Litigation by terminated employees, most often on the basis of the discrimination laws, is common. While Minnesota courts will usually affirm the layoff decision in the absence of some additional showing of discrimination, the impact of the decision on individual jobs should be examined to see that the employer's action will withstand challenge.[419]

Employers reducing their workforces by instituting layoffs or RIFs should attempt to minimize a disproportionately large adverse impact on any protected group (age, sex, race, disability, etc.). Protected employees may be adversely affected in disproportionately large numbers when RIFs occur unless employers plan in advance to assure that their pattern of layoffs is not discriminatory. For example, if ten positions are to be eliminated and seven of those positions are held by women over age 50, the employer should re-evaluate its plan to see whether, through transfers or other alternatives, the adverse impact on the protected group members can be reduced.

Reductions in force may have a disproportionate, adverse impact and can often lead to discrimination claims. When this outcome is likely to occur, an employer should try to identify a plan which reduces or eliminates such impact yet accomplishes its legitimate goal of reducing costs.

Typically, employers consider the following objective factors in their RIF decisions: the positions to be eliminated, the skills required to perform the remaining jobs, the seniority of the available employees, and the past performance of employees. If the employer's objective criteria are documented in advance and the employer can demonstrate that these objective and nondiscriminatory reasons resulted in the terminations, the layoffs will probably be defensible as nondiscriminatory in the face of discrimination challenges.

PLANT CLOSING LAWS

The federal plant closing law, the WARN Act, requires a 60-day advance notice to employees who will be affected by either a plant closing or a mass layoff.[420] To be covered under WARN, the employer must have, in total (including all companies which are part of the same controlled group), at least 100 full-time employees. The plant closing or mass layoff must consist of employment loss for at least 50 full-time employees at a single site of employment. For a mass layoff (where the facility will remain open), the 50 full-time employees must constitute at least one-third of the active workforce at that site. The layoffs need not occur all at once, but may be considered all part of one action, covered by WARN, if they occur within a 30-day period or, if there are a number of smaller layoffs (each one under 50) which together total at least 50, in a 90-day period.

Employers providing federal WARN Act notice must also report the names, addresses and occupations of all employees being terminated to the Minnesota Commissioner of Employment and Economic Development.[421]

There are strict statutory requirements concerning the information which must be provided to affected employees, union representatives, and Minnesota state and local government officials. Fines and penalties can be imposed upon employers who fail to comply with the notice requirements; however, there are also exceptions which permit employers under certain circumstances to provide fewer than 60-days advance notice or no notice at all. Dislocated workers may qualify for certain benefits under state law.

Any employer with at least 100 employees should consult with legal counsel if the employer will be laying off at least 50 employees at any single site during a 90-day period.

EMPLOYMENT AT WILL

Minnesota recognizes the rule of "employment at-will." That means, in the absence of a collective bargaining agreement or other employment contract, an employer can discharge an employee at any time for any legal reason, with or without notice, and the employee can resign at any time for any reason, with or without notice. An employer should include "at-will" language in its employee handbook and should require the employee, at hire, to sign an acknowledgment that the employee understands the "at-will" nature of the relationship.

The employment relationship will generally remain "at-will" unless the employer does something to change it. Employers can unintentionally eliminate or modify an employee's "at-will" status, thereby restricting their ability to terminate an employee at any time, by doing the following:

- An employer "contracts" with an employee (orally or in writing) that employment will be of a certain duration or, if termination is permitted under the contract, that it can occur only under specified circumstances.

- An employee handbook that limits the circumstances in which the employer can terminate the employee's employment can create an employment contract. Careful drafting of handbooks will prevent this inadvertent consequence.

- An employer may make promises to the employee upon which the employee relies. For example, if the employer induces the employee to take an assignment out of town promising "this reassignment will only last a year," the employee moves, and then the employer terminates the employee, the employer may have destroyed the at will relationship for the "promised" year.

Although most employees are employed at-will and can be terminated for any legal reason, they cannot be terminated for an illegal, discriminatory, or retaliatory reason, including the following:

- **Age Discrimination Laws**. It is unlawful for an employer to discharge an employee because of that person's age. Minnesota law protects persons over the age of majority (18); the federal Age Discrimination in Employment Act protects persons age 40 and older.

  Minnesota law also requires that an employer give 30-days notice of its intention to terminate an employee who is 65 years of age or older (earlier than age 70) on the grounds that he or she can no longer meet the requirements of the job.[422]

- **The Minnesota Human Rights Act**,[423] **Title VII of the Civil Rights Act**. It is unlawful for an employer to discharge an individual because of the individual's race, color, creed, religion, sex, national origin, age, disability, marital status, sexual orientation, membership or activity in a local commission, or status with regard to public assistance. These laws prohibit discharge or other adverse employment action against employees who either file complaints under these laws or participate as witnesses in investigations of claims under these laws.

- **The Americans with Disabilities Act**.[424] It is unlawful for an employer to discharge an employee because of that person's disability.

- **Federal and Minnesota Fair Labor Standards Acts**.[425] It is unlawful for an employer to discharge an employee for complaining about minimum wages, overtime pay or other wage-related claims.

- **Federal and Minnesota Labor Management Relations Acts**.[426] It is unlawful for an employer to discharge an employee for union activity, protected concerted activity or complaining, filing or giving testimony under these laws.

- **Federal and State OSHA (Occupational Safety and Health Acts)**.[427] It is unlawful for an employer to discharge an employee for exercising rights under these laws.

- **Workers' Compensation Statute**.[428] It is unlawful for an employer to discharge an employee for seeking workers' compensation benefits.

- **ERISA (Employee Retirement Income Security Act)**.[429] An employer may not discharge an employee for asserting pension or other benefit rights under this law or for testifying under this law, and it may not prevent an employee from attaining rights under any employee benefit plan.

- **The Minnesota Parental Leave Law; the Federal Family and Medical Leave Act**.[430] It is unlawful for an employer to discharge or retaliate against any eligible employee who exercises his or her right to take unpaid parental leave or family and medical leave.

- **Charitable Fund Drives**.[431] An employer may not discharge or retaliate against an employee who fails to participate in a charitable drive.

- **Garnishment**.[432] It is unlawful for an employer to discharge an employee whose wages have been subject to garnishment.

- **Reporting Child Abuse**.[433] It is unlawful for an employer to discharge an employee who is required to report child abuse for making such a report.

- **Strike Participation**.[434] It is unlawful for an employer to discharge a person in retaliation for that person participating in a strike.

- **Whistle Blower Statute**.[435] An employer may not discharge, discipline or discriminate against an employee because the employee or a person acting on behalf of an employee reported in good faith a violation or suspected violation of any federal or state law to an employer or to any governmental body or law enforcement official. An employer may also not discipline, discharge or discriminate against an employee for refusing to participate in any activity that the employee believes violated any state or federal law, rule, or regulation.

- **Jury Duty**.[436] It is unlawful for an employer to discharge an employee because that employee receives a summons, serves as a juror, or attends court for prospective jury service.

- **Access to Personnel Files**.[437] An employer may not discharge or retaliate against eligible employees who seek to exercise their access rights under this law.

Note that employees are protected not only against discharge but against all types of adverse employment action suffered due to the exercise of their rights under these laws. The above list contains common examples of laws which prohibit employers from taking discriminatory or retaliatory actions against employees.

THE TERMINATION PROCESS

Prior to terminating an employee, the employer should review a checklist, such as the following, to minimize exposure to legal claims. This list is illustrative, not exhaustive:

- Does the employee's status as a member of a protected class enter into or appear to enter into the decision to terminate, either directly or indirectly? (For example, terminating an employee on FMLA leave, even if it is for good cause, will raise an automatic question of discriminatory motive.)

- Are any factors involved which may make it appear as though the employee was discharged in retaliation for exercising a legal right, satisfying a legal obligation, or opposing or refusing to assist in unlawful employer activities?

- Does the employee have a disability? Is he or she a member of a protected class?

- Is the employee engaged in protected union activity?

- How long has the employee been employed? If for a short term, was the employee recruited from other employment or out of town? Were any representations made regarding job security?

- Are there any documents describing the employee's terms and conditions of employment, such as employment contracts or offer letters?

- Are there any performance evaluations or is there a progressive discipline policy? If so, what do such documents say?

- Have complaints been documented and given to the employee?

- Has the employee been warned that failure to correct deficiencies may lead to termination?

- Does the employer have written termination procedures in a policy manual? Have they been followed?

- What is the reason for the discharge? Is the reason supported by documentation? Has the reason been conveyed to the employee?

- Are any employee benefits (such as stock options, pension eligibility, longevity bonus) about to vest for the employee?

- Do the circumstances warrant disciplinary action other than termination?

- Is the proposed termination consistent with the company's action in similar circumstances in the past?

Also be aware of the following:

- Does this termination involve a public policy situation (e.g., employee just finished jury duty or military service)? Has the employee reported a violation of the law or filed a complaint with a governmental agency?

- Have written personnel policies setting forth standards of fairness been followed (e.g., was the employee fired in anger)?

- Have significant contingent benefits not yet vested (e.g., commissions, profit sharing or pension benefits)?

- Is the reason for the termination going to be difficult to prove?

If any of the above warning signals appear, the employer should consider either delaying the termination or negotiating a separation agreement with the employee which includes a release of the employee's claims. A release is a legal document that should be drafted by legal counsel. If there is no apparent liability, after consulting with legal counsel and reviewing the points listed above, and the employer decides to proceed with the termination, the following guidelines may be helpful:

- **Be fair**. Fairness is the best preventive measure. Most employees sue because they feel they have been treated unfairly.

- **Be candid**. Do not depart from the truth (e.g., in oral representations or written evaluations). For example, do not give "job elimination" as a reason if you merely intend to shift job titles. This is critical in view of a United States Supreme Court decision holding that proof that an employer has given a false reason for terminating an employee may be sufficient for a discharged employee to prevail in a discrimination suit brought against the employer.[438] This is also important in view of Minnesota's Notice of Termination law, described later in this Guide.[439] Further, do not give poor performance as a reason if there are no unsatisfactory job evaluations and the real reason involves something else. You should have clear, concise reasons for the termination. If you do not, this should serve as a check on whether the decision is a sound one. Treat the employee with respect, emphasizing what he or she has done for the company in the past without being sympathetic or giving false hope about future opportunities. Also, do not be defensive about the decision.

- **Be consistent**. For example, if an internal rating system is set up, use it in all cases. Inconsistency damages an employer's credibility, and credibility is necessary for a legally defensible position.

- **Be definite.** A business decision has been made, and that decision should be clearly communicated to the employee.

- **Be informative.** Have all the information you need to assist the employee in making this change, e.g., final wage information, vacation pay, commissions, retirement benefits, severance pay (there is no statutory or common law requirement for this), group insurance benefits, health continuation coverage, outplacement or employee assistance programs, etc. If you are helpful in this regard, it will add to the employee's feeling of being treated fairly. If you give no guidance, the employee may feel lost and turn to an attorney for assistance.

- **Be discreet.** Notification to the employee should be private, at a time and place which will avoid unnecessary embarrassment or claims of defamation. Information regarding the reasons for termination should not be disseminated more broadly than is absolutely necessary to carry out the discharge.

RELEASE AGREEMENTS

If the employer may potentially incur liability for terminating an employee, the employer should reevaluate the termination decision. If the employer wishes to proceed in spite of potential liability, the employer may consider offering to provide the employee with severance benefits in exchange for a release of all claims against the employer. A release agreement should be professionally drafted but written in plain English, and the employee should be given sufficient time to consider it.

Employers should be aware that a waiver of claims under the Minnesota Human Rights Act ("MHRA") must include a notice to the employee of his or her right to rescind the agreement within 15 days after the employee signs the agreement. Specific rescission language is required by the MHRA.[440] In addition, the employer is reminded that a waiver of claims under the Age Discrimination in Employment Act requires both a 21-day review period prior to execution of the release (45 days where two or more employee offered termination package) and a seven-day revocation period after execution of the release, as well as certain required disclosures which must be contained in the release.[441] See Waiver of Rights Under the Age Discrimination Laws elsewhere in this Guide.

If the employee agrees to sign a release, it must be supported by something beyond what he or she is already entitled to by law or company policy. The consideration does not have to be only monetary; it can include a positive employment reference, outplacement counseling, or a release of the employer's claims against the employee. It is unlawful to threaten criminal prosecution if the employee does not sign a release.[442] Further, the release should:

- Be voluntarily and knowingly given (i.e., the employee must be aware of what he or she is signing);

- Be as specific as possible with respect to the consideration given by the employer;

- Recite that the employee was given the opportunity to consult with legal counsel;

- Disclaim any wrongdoing on the part of the company;

- Release all known and unknown claims against the employer which the employee has or may have up to the time the agreement is signed;

- Contain a nondisclosure clause; and

- If applicable, contain notice of the 15 and 7-day rights of rescission and specific ADEA requirements, including the 21 or 45-day review period.

SEVERANCE PAY POLICIES AS ERISA PLANS

Employers who establish severance "policies" under which severance is regularly paid to terminating employees should know that such policies may constitute "employee benefit plans" subject to the requirements of the Employee Retirement Income Security Act (ERISA). This may be the case even though the employer's severance policy is unwritten, or even though the employer only pays severance under particular circumstances. Severance packages offered to employees in connection with a reduction in force may also be subject to ERISA.

ERISA's reporting, disclosure, and fiduciary requirements are complex, and the penalties for failure to comply with ERISA are potentially significant. (See Employee Benefit Plans, ERISA, and the Internal Revenue Code section of this Guide on explanations relating to penalties). In addition, employers whose severance policies are ERISA plans may subject themselves to the risk of litigation by former employees who did not receive, but believe they are entitled to, severance pay based on the employer's past practices. Employers who have severance policies, or who regularly pay severance to some or all of their terminated employees, should seek the advice of legal counsel in determining the extent to which their severance arrangements may be subject to ERISA.

PAYMENT OF TERMINATED EMPLOYEES' WAGES

Employers must pay discharged employees within 24 hours of their demand for wages.[443] If the employer does not pay within 24 hours of demand, the employer may be liable for a penalty of up to 15 days of additional wages. The employer must make the wages available at the usual place of payment unless the employee requests payment through the mail. If the employee requests payment by mail, the wages are considered paid as of the date of the postmark.[444]

Employees who resign are entitled to be paid their wages or commissions earned by the employer's next regular payday. However, if resignation occurs less than five days before the next regular payday then the employee must be paid the second regular payday after resignation. In any event, the employee must be paid within 20 days.[445] The penalty to an employer for failing to provide payment within this time period is payment of up to 15 days of additional wages. Special rules apply for the payment of wages to resigning migrant workers.

Employers must also pay commissions to salespersons who are paid on a commission basis and who are independent contractors and not employees, when either the salesperson or the employer terminates the relationship. If the employer terminates the salesperson or if the salesperson resigns with at least five days written notice, the employer must pay commissions earned through the last day of employment on demand no later than three working days after the salesperson's last day of work.[446] If the salesperson resigns without five days' written notice, the employer must pay commissions earned through the last day of employment on demand no later than six working days after the salesperson's last day of work. For these purposes, the term "commissions earned through the last day of employment" means commissions due for services or merchandise which have actually been delivered to and accepted by the customer by the final day of the salespersons' employment. If the employer fails to pay the commissions within the times specified, the employer is liable not only for the unpaid commission, but also for a penalty in an amount equal to 1/15 of the salesperson's commissions earned through the last day of employment, for each day up to fifteen days that the commissions go unpaid, plus attorney's fees.

If the discharged or resigning employee or salesperson was entrusted with the handling of money or property during his or her employ, the employer has ten working days after the termination of employment to audit or adjust the person's accounts before wages or commissions are payable. No penalties will accrue during this ten-day period.

Note that the law does not require that a salesperson collect commissions on merchandise ordered prior to the last day of employment but delivered and accepted after termination.

NOTICE OF REASON FOR TERMINATION

Within fifteen working days after an employee has been involuntarily terminated, the employee may make a written request to the employer for a written explanation of the truthful reasons for termination.[447] Within ten working days after receiving the request for explanation, the employer must inform the terminated employee in writing of the truthful reason for the termination. No communication of the statement furnished by the employer to the employee under this law may be made the subject of an action for libel, slander or defamation by the employee against the employer.

Employers should notify employees of the right to obtain the reason for their termination by posting the appropriate Minnesota poster.

REFERENCES

Until recently, Minnesota employers were generally advised to adopt a policy of not communicating any information about former employees to prospective employers or to any other person, other than the dates of the employee's employment and positions held by the employee. Minnesota law[448] now permits private employers to provide the information about employees or former employees without being subject to a legal claim by the employee.

The following information can be provided by an employer without written authorization from the employee:

(1) dates of employment;
(2) compensation and wage history;
(3) job description and duties;
(4) training and education provided by the employer;
(5) acts of violence, theft, harassment, or illegal conduct documented in the personnel record that resulted in disciplinary action, termination or resignation. If the employee submitted a written response to the action, that must be supplied as well.

Information disclosed in (5) above must also be sent to the employee at their last address. Additionally, if the employee provides written authorization, the employer may disclose the following in addition to the items listed above:

(6) written evaluations and employee's response;
(7) written disciplinary warnings/actions in the employee's file, in the last 5 years and the employee's written response;
(8) written reasons for separation.

Responses to these items must also be mailed to the employee at the same time as it is mailed to the person requesting the information.

Public employers are generally protected from liability under the Minnesota Data Practices Act[449] if the employee gives written consent to provide:

(1) employee evaluations and any written response contained in personnel record;
(2) written reasons for separation from employment.

An employer may still decline to provide information on former employees, but should have a written policy advising employees of this policy.

Supervisory and management personnel should be directed to refer all calls for references to one person, such as the human resources director or person acting in that capacity. Other supervisory and management personnel should be directed not to discuss a former employee with any outside person or even within the company.

Supervisory personnel often freely converse with people looking for information, potentially to the great detriment of the employer. The supervisor could be held to have acted on behalf of the employer and to have defamed or invaded the privacy of former employees. Such problems can be avoided if supervisory personnel are adequately trained and reference requests are handled properly.

TERMINATING INDEPENDENT SALES REPRESENTATIVES

Minnesota law[450] prohibits termination of a sales representative agreement during its term unless the principal (the represented manufacturer, wholesaler, assembler or importer) has good cause. The law permits non-renewal of a sales representative agreement without good cause, but requires specified notice. By its terms, the law applies to sales representatives who, during some part of the period of the agreement, were residents of Minnesota or whose geographic territory specified in the sales agreement included part or all of Minnesota.[451] The law applies only to independent contractors, and it has the following features:

- "Good cause" for termination includes but is not limited to:

  - A material breach of a written sales representative agreement;

  - If there is no written agreement, failure by the sales representative to substantially comply with material, reasonable requirements imposed by the principal;

  - The sales representative's bankruptcy or insolvency;

  - Assignment of the sales representative's assets for the benefit of creditors;

  - Voluntary abandonment of the business;

  - Conviction or a plea of guilty or no contest to a charge of violating a law relating to the sales representative's business;

  - Other conduct that materially impairs the good will associated with the principal's trademark, trade name, or other commercial symbol; or

  - Failure to forward customer payments to the principal.

- The principal must give the sales representative 90-days advance written notice of the intent to terminate and the reasons for termination. In most cases the sales representative has 60 days from receipt of the notice to correct the reasons given for the termination. The termination notice may be effective immediately upon receipt, however, in certain defined instances.

- Sales representatives protected by the law are persons who contract with a principal to solicit wholesale orders and who are compensated in whole or in part by commissions. The law excludes persons who are employees of the principal; who place orders or purchase for their own account for resale; who hold goods on a consignment basis for their own account for resale; or who distribute, sell, or offer goods other than samples to end users, not for resale (i.e., retailers).

- Upon termination of the sales representative agreement, the sales representative is entitled to be paid for all sales as to which the representative would have been entitled to commissions pursuant to the provisions of the sales representative agreement made prior to the later of the termination date or the end of the notice period, regardless of whether the goods or services are actually delivered to the customer. Commissions are due in accordance with the terms of the sales representative agreement or as otherwise provided by law.

- If the principal wishes to end its sales representative agreement by not renewing it, it must give written notice of intent not to renew at least 90 days prior to expiration of an agreement with a set expiration date. In the case of an agreement with no expiration date, notice of intent not to renew shall cause the agreement to terminate 180 days after the notice of intent not to renew. The principal does not have to have good cause to not renew a sales representative relationship. If the failure to renew is for good cause, and the sales representative has failed to correct the reasons communicated to him as set forth above, compliance with this provision is not required.

Claims by the principal involving alleged violations of this statute must be resolved by arbitration. The sales representative may submit the matter for arbitration or may sue in court prior to the arbitration hearing. Both parties are bound by the arbitration, and generally must bear the costs of arbitration equally. Remedies that may be awarded by the arbitrator include sustaining the termination, reinstatement of the agreement or damages, and payment of commissions. The prevailing party may, in some cases, recover costs and attorneys' fees, including the full amount of the arbitrator's fee and expenses.

UNEMPLOYMENT COMPENSATION/INSURANCE

OVERVIEW

Both federal and Minnesota law require that most employers who employ individuals within the state of Minnesota contribute unemployment taxes to the federal and state unemployment insurance fund. Employers contribute to the state-administered fund through a system of payroll taxes. The purpose of the fund is to provide temporary partial wage replacement to employees who have lost their jobs through no fault of their own and who, although able, have not found suitable reemployment. The program is known as the Minnesota Unemployment Insurance Program.[452]

The collection of unemployment taxes and the administration of unemployment insurance benefits for workers is governed by the Minnesota Unemployment Insurance Law (the "Act").[453] Administration of the Act is the responsibility of the Minnesota Department of Employment and Economic Development (the "Department"). Its main office is located at 332 Minnesota Street, Suite E200, St. Paul, Minnesota 55101. The Department is helpful in providing information to employers about their liability and will answer questions that generally arise under the Act. The Department's web site is: www.deed.state.mn.us, or www.uimn.org.

Employers come in contact with the Department quarterly when they determine and pay their unemployment taxes; annually when their experience rating (used to determine the amount of taxes due) is determined; and each time an employer acquires or disposes of part or all of a business.

Employers also come in contact with the Department each time an employee terminates employment, whether voluntarily or involuntarily, and files a claim for unemployment insurance benefits. For many employers, the award or denial of unemployment insurance benefits is their first and most frequent adversarial process involving employees. In some instances, the unemployment benefits claims procedure is the first step toward (and may influence) later litigation between the employer and employee arising out of the employee's employment and termination.

EMPLOYERS COVERED BY THE ACT

Generally, most employers[454] will be required to pay unemployment taxes for all of their employees unless specifically exempted under the Act. The tax is figured as a percentage of a fixed dollar amount of each employee's wages.

Special rules apply to covered agricultural employment,[455] non-covered domestic employment,[456] and construction/independent contractors.[457] There are several categories of covered employers, including businesses for profit, nonprofit organizations, governmental entities, joint ventures, and religious, charitable or educational institutions. There are also non-covered employers who voluntarily elect to be covered under the Act.[458] A person whose work force consists of 50 percent or more of workers provided by employee leasing firms is jointly and severally liable for unpaid taxes.[459]

When an employer acquires a significant portion or all of an organization, trade or business, or the workforce of another covered business, and there is 25 percent or more common ownership or there is substantially common management or control between the predecessor and successor employer, the successor employer will assume the experience rating history (described below) of the business (or the portion thereof) acquired.[460] Common ownership includes ownership by spouse, parent, grandparent, child, grandchild, brother, sister, aunt, uncle, niece, nephew or first cousin by birth or by marriage. Successor employers have the responsibility to notify the Department of the acquisition by electronic transmission within 30 calendar days of the date of acquisition, or the employer may face penalties.

Depending on the structure of the businesses (i.e., whether organized and operated separately or together as a single entity), a single rate or separate rates could be charged to businesses under common control. Finally, special rules apply to employees who perform services in several states to determine in which state taxes must be paid.

Corporate officers, directors and employees with responsibility for payment of unemployment taxes and filing the appropriate tax reports incur personal liability for taxes or reimbursements if they pay other creditors knowing such tax payments remain unpaid, without regard to motive or intent.[461] Such personal liability is avoidable only in personal bankruptcy. Further, any partner of an L.L.P. or P.L.L.P. is jointly and severally liable for these taxes or reimbursements in the event the employer does not pay.[462]

EMPLOYEES COVERED BY THE ACT

Most forms of employment are covered by the Act.[463] All individuals performing services for an employer other than independent contractors will generally be covered employees, with certain exceptions. This includes officers of a corporation, members of a limited liability company (LLC) who generally would be considered employees of the LLC, commission drivers distributing certain products, and certain traveling and city salespersons. Temporary and part-time employees may be covered under the Act.

Independent contractors are not engaged in employment within the meaning of the Act.[464] As discussed earlier, an employer may wish to treat a person as an independent contractor rather than an employee to avoid responsibility for, among other items, payment of unemployment taxes. Before treating any individual as an independent contractor, however, employers should seek the advice of legal counsel. Independent contractor issues often arise in the unemployment context when an individual files a claim for unemployment insurance benefits on the ground that he or she was a bona fide employee and not an independent contractor at the time of termination. The Department may, in addition, investigate the status of independent contractors on its own initiative.

There are several additional categories of employees who are not covered by the Act,[465] including:

- Commission-only real estate and insurance salespersons.

- Ministers of a church, church employees, and members of religious orders or organizations, including related entities operated primarily for religious purposes, unless the organization opts for coverage under the Act.

- Domestic employees paid less than $1,000 in each calendar quarter.

- Students employed by the educational institution at which they are enrolled.

- Interns in the employ of a hospital, if the individual has completed a four-year course in an accredited medical school.

- Agricultural labor on farms in which calendar year quarterly wages total less than $20,000 or fewer than four persons over age 16 worked fewer than 20 weeks in a calendar year.

- Corporate officers, if the officer owns 25% or more of the employer corporation.

- Members of a limited liability company, if the member owns 25% or more of the LLC.

DETERMINATION AND PAYMENT OF UNEMPLOYMENT TAXES

New or first time employers in Minnesota are charged an unemployment tax rate as set by the Commissioner.[466] This rate may change from year to year depending on the amount of benefits paid and the taxable wages for all contributing employers. Employers should contact the Department in order to determine the exact tax rate. In addition, employers should note that employers who have paid the state unemployment tax receive a credit that lowers the amount of federal unemployment taxes. (For more information refer to the Minnesota Department of Employment and Economic Development's website at www.deed.state.mn.us or www.uimn.org/tax).

A minimum rate is added to each employer's experience rating, representing the cost of the insurance fund not included in the experience rating, plus the additional cost to provide programs for dislocated workers. Since the solvency of the fund fluctuates depending on economic conditions, the state has the authority to impose a tax surcharge if the fund drops below a certain level. The minimum rate may be reduced if the fund exceeds certain levels.

Wages are defined to include all remuneration for services, including among other items, cash wages, salary, commissions, bonuses, tips and gratuities paid to an employee by a customer of an employer and accounted for by the employee to the employer, S corporation dividends (when credited to shareholders for services), and the reasonable value of meals and housing provided to an employee. Also included are wages contributed to a "401(k)" plan (cash or deferred salary reduction profit sharing plan) and a "cafeteria" or flexible benefit plan.[467]

Certain payments are not included in the definitions of wages, among which are retirement, long term disability and disability workers' compensation payments and certain other sickness or accident disability payments.

Unemployment insurance benefits paid to an employee are charged to those employers who employed the person during the first four of the five completed calendar quarters immediately prior to the effective date of an applicant's benefit account (base period). Each base period employer is notified that an application has been made for benefits. However, if a base period employer was not liable for benefits to an employee based on the circumstances of the termination from that employer (such as employment misconduct of the employee), any application involving that employee would not be charged against that employer's account.[468]

After June 30 of each year, an employer's experience rating is redetermined. The new rate applies to all taxable wages paid during the next calendar year. An employer may "buy down" the new rate by making a lump sum payment at the beginning of each year. The lump sum payment is generally equal to 125 percent of the unemployment benefits used to determine the experience rating. This may lower an employer's unemployment tax cost for the next year, especially if the employer's payroll has grown substantially.[469]

Certain forms, available from the Department, are required to be filed by new employers and by buyers and sellers of businesses. Quarterly forms are also required for the reporting of wages and the payment of taxes. Penalties and interest are charged for late payment and late reports. A detailed discussion of these requirements is beyond the scope of this Guide; however, a general discussion may be found in the publication "A Guide to Starting a Business in Minnesota," available from the Minnesota Small Business Assistance Office. The guide is available online at www.deed.state. mn.us/publications/index.htm#bus. You may also access Minnesota's Unemployment Insurance website (www.uimn.org) and download the "Employer Handbook" which will answer many employer questions.

BENEFIT ELIGIBILITY

To be eligible for unemployment benefits, an applicant must establish a benefit account that requires:

- High quarter wage credits of at least $1000; and

- Wage credits, in other than the high quarter, of at least $250.[470]

Procedurally, to be eligible for benefits an employee must file an application for benefits with the Department. The Department will notify the employer that an application has been made. The employer will then have an opportunity to explain why, if applicable, the employee should be disqualified from benefits. An applicant is entitled to benefits if:

- The termination was through no fault of the applicant;

- The applicant has an active benefit account and has filed a continued biweekly request for unemployment benefits. The applicant has served a waiting period of one week (benefits are not paid for the first week of unemployment);

- The applicant reports periodically as required to determine the availability of suitable work;

- The employee is actively seeking work and, if applicable, is participating in reemployment services such as a job search assistance program; and

- The employee is able and willing to accept suitable work, including suitable reemployment with any prior base period employer.

If any condition is not met, the applicant is not entitled to benefits or the continuation of benefits.[471]

The dollar amount of weekly benefits is based on a percentage of the applicant's average weekly wage, subject to a maximum based on a percentage of average weekly wages paid statewide. Benefits are payable for up to 26 weeks or until one-third of base period wages have been paid as benefits, whichever is less. Emergency federal legislation may provide extended benefits beyond the 26-week maximum.

The employee may obtain temporary or part-time work and still receive benefits, as long as the temporary or part-time work is less than 32 hours regardless of the amount of any earnings. Earnings from such employment may, however, offset benefits paid.[472] Employees may now also accept employment in a new occupation or trade on a trial basis; if the employee finds he or she is not suitable for the new occupation or trade and quits within 30 days of the start, the employee may resume receiving benefits. Similarly, dislocated workers (those whose opportunities in suitable employment are limited) who are awaiting job retraining may accept temporary employment and resume benefits once training begins.

Even though an employee may meet all of the above conditions, under certain circumstances, he or she may not be eligible immediately to receive unemployment insurance benefits, e.g., if the employee has received or is receiving certain payments, including:

- Accrued vacation pay;

- Holiday pay;

- Workers' compensation benefits;

- Old-age benefits under Social Security (50 percent exclusion);

- Primary Social Security disability benefits;

- Pension benefits from the employer;

- Severance benefits; or

- Back pay

DISQUALIFICATION FROM BENEFITS

An applicant is entitled to benefits so long as the termination or other employment action was not due to the applicant's own fault. Under the Act, there are several reasons why the applicant would not qualify, including his or her:

- Aggravated misconduct;

- Misconduct;

- Voluntary termination (e.g., "quit") without good cause attributable to the employer;

- Voluntary leave of absence (medical leave not presumed to be voluntary);

- Suspension from employment without pay as a result of employment misconduct;

- Failure to apply for or accept suitable work;

- Refusing an offer of suitable reemployment by a base period employer; or

- Participating in a labor strike.

Most of the court cases interpreting the Act involve whether misconduct is of such a nature to disqualify a claimant from receipt of unemployment benefits or whether a quit was without good cause attributable to the employer such that the claimant is disqualified from receiving unemployment benefits.

AGGRAVATED MISCONDUCT

Aggravated misconduct is defined as assault and battery, malicious destruction of property, arson, sabotage, embezzlement, financial exploitation or any other act which amounts to a felony or gross misdemeanor under criminal laws if the act interfered with or adversely affected the employment. An employee who commits aggravated misconduct will not only be disqualified from benefits, but will lose any wage credits attributable to that employer. In that way, the employer will not be charged for any benefits payable as a result of a subsequent termination of employment where such employer is among the base period employers.

MISCONDUCT

Misconduct is defined as any intentional, negligent or indifferent conduct, on or off the job, that (1) shows a serious violation of the standards of behavior the employer has the right to reasonably expect of the employee, or (2) shows a substantial lack of concern for the employment.[473] Misconduct commonly falls into one of the following categories:

- Deliberate violation of rules;

- Deliberate disregard of standard behavior that the employer has a right to expect;

- Gross carelessness or gross negligence; or

- Lack of concern for one's job.

Intent may be obvious in certain types of conduct, such as stealing or falsifying records. In other situations, however, intent may not be obvious. For example, the employee may be involved in a series of related or unrelated acts, each of which alone is not misconduct, but which, in the aggregate, show a lack of concern for one's job. The following is a short list of acts that courts have found, based on the specific facts presented, may constitute misconduct to deny benefits:

- Sleeping on the job;

- Fighting (except in self defense);

- Horseplay;

- Violation of major work rules;

- Unauthorized leaving of work, either a single instance causing immediate harm or a series of instances;

- Excessive or unauthorized absenteeism and tardiness within the employee's control. (Courts favor those employers that have given prior notice to the employee that excessive or unauthorized absenteeism and tardiness may result in discharge to show either the employee's intent or lack of concern from subsequent absences);

- Insubordination, including refusing a reasonable employer request or violating standards of behavior;

- Failure to cooperate with a performance improvement plan;

- Use of alcohol or drugs during working hours;

- Sexual or other harassment by the employee against others;

- Certain off-duty conduct that affects the employee's ability to perform the job; and

- The "last straw" doctrine, in which a series of minor work rule violations or other related or unrelated acts, culminating in a single serious act, will demonstrate such lack of concern for the employer's well being as to constitute misconduct.

Some acts by the employee, although serious or harmful to the employer, may not rise to a level of misconduct under the Act and do not result in a disqualification from benefits. For example:

- Inefficiency or unsatisfactory performance;

- Failure to perform due to inability;

- Good faith error in judgment;

- Actions arising out of inadequate instructions or miscommunication attributable to employer;

- Violation of policies or rules of which the employer failed to give the employee adequate notice;

- Absence because of illness or injury with proper notice to the employer; and

- Conduct directly resulting from an employee's chemical dependency unless the employee was previously diagnosed chemically dependent, or had treatment for chemical dependency and since diagnosis or treatment has failed to make consistent efforts to control the chemical dependency.

VOLUNTARY TERMINATION

A voluntary termination (i.e. a "quit") will disqualify an employee from unemployment benefits, provided the quit was truly voluntary and not the result of good cause attributable to the employer. For example, an employee who quits to avoid being terminated has actually been terminated if the employer gives the employee an ultimatum ("quit or I'll fire you"). Closing of a financially troubled business may not disqualify the owner employee from receiving benefits on the basis of a voluntary quit.

Under the Act, an employee will not be disqualified even if the termination is voluntary if it generally results from, among other circumstances, the following:

- The employee's serious illness or injury that makes it medically necessary that the employee quit, provided that the employee informs the employer of the serious illness or injury and requests accommodation and no reasonable accommodation was made available; or

- The employee's loss of child care for a minor child caused the employee to quit employment, provided the employee made reasonable efforts to obtain other child care and requested time off or other accommodation from the employer and no reasonable accommodation was made available.

In addition, good cause attributable to the employer will justify a voluntary quit and not disqualify an employee from benefits. Examples of good cause would generally include:

- Sexual harassment directed against the employee, about which the employer knows or should have known and failed to prevent;

- A substantial (generally at least 20 percent) reduction in total pay or benefits;

- A substantial increase or change in the hours of work or duties assigned to the employee without his or her consent (does not include shift changes that should have been anticipated by the employee as part of the employment);

- Employer misconduct such as violation of an employee's contract, an employer's own policies on discipline, or an employer's request that an employee violate a law or regulation.

On the other hand, good cause attributable to the employer would generally not occur in the following circumstances:

- Modest decrease (15% or less) in wages or benefits;

- A reasonable change in work hours or shift;

- Change in the commission structure (unless it results in a substantial reduction in pay);

- Transportation problems of the employee;

- Demotion after prior warning; or

- Disagreements involving issues related to policy or personality.

Courts constantly review and interpret these standards in a variety of fact situations. There are numerous decisions interpreting each of these general categories. In deciding whether to challenge an employee's right to unemployment insurance benefits, employers are advised to assemble all of the facts and determine whether an employee's conduct fits within one of the categories described above such as misconduct or voluntary quit not attributable to the employer. Certain situations will obviously result in a denial of benefits; others will obviously result in the granting of benefits. It is, however, those "gray areas" which should be reviewed with legal counsel, who may be able to find similar cases that would be instructive on how the Department or the court may decide the issue.

BENEFIT DETERMINATION AND APPEAL PROCEDURE

The employer has ten days after receipt of notice from the Department of an employee or former employee's claim for benefits to file a wage statement protesting the employee or former employee's entitlement to benefits. This protest should contain as complete and accurate a statement of the facts as possible and should include all relevant reasons (under the Act) in support of the disqualification.

The Department will then make an initial determination, based on the written statements, whether to grant or deny benefits. Each party will receive notice of the Department's determination. The losing party may appeal by sending written notice of appeal within 20 days of the notice of the determination.[474] If an appeal from the initial determination is taken, a telephonic administrative hearing is held to gather additional evidence.[475] The Department has published rules on the conduct of such hearings.[476] The hearing procedure is somewhat informal, and the typical rules of evidence and trial procedure are liberalized. An unemployment insurance judge conducts the hearing, which is tape recorded. Attorneys may be present at the hearing. Each party, employer and employee/former employee, must bring all evidence, including documents and witnesses, necessary to establish its case.

The party with the greater weight of evidence will prevail on the issues which it has the burden of proving. For example, the employer has the burden of proving that the employee/former employee is disqualified, that the termination was voluntary, or that the termination was due to the employee's misconduct. A former employee has the burden of proving that a voluntary quit was for good cause attributable to the employer. Each party has an opportunity to cross-examine witnesses and to bring forth evidence rebutting the claims of the other party.

The transcript developed from this hearing will be used in any later appeal to the Minnesota Court of Appeals. Therefore, the hearing is an employer's best opportunity to make a complete record that the employee/former employee should be denied benefits.

The party that does not prevail after the administrative hearing has 20 days from the notice of the unemployment law judge's determination to file a request for reconsideration asking the unemployment law judge who made the determination to reconsider that decision, stating the reason why the determination should be reversed.[477] The Department will then send a notice to all parties involved stating that the request for reconsideration has been filed. Involved parties have the right to comment on the request for reconsideration and have the right to receive recorded testimony or exhibits from the evidentiary hearing. In some cases, the unemployment law judge may order an additional evidentiary hearing. Further appeal from an unemployment law judge's final decision would be to the Minnesota Court of Appeals, which would decide legal issues involving the standards for review or interpret one of the qualifying or disqualifying events.

If the employer is successful in reversing an initial determination of eligibility either at the hearing or upon the request for reconsideration level, any benefits previously paid to the employee/former employee will not be charged against the employer. In that case, the employee/former employee will be denied further benefits until he or she again accepts and is later terminated from covered employment and must, in addition, repay any amount previously paid. The only exception to the repayment requirement is if the unemployment law judge upheld the initial determination and that decision was reversed upon request for reconsideration or upon appeal to the Court of Appeals.

Employers should be cautious in contesting a claim for unemployment insurance benefits, especially if the employer anticipates that the employee/former employee may sue the employer over events leading up to a termination or voluntary quit, since the employee/former employee may obtain information during the hearing process more easily than in later litigation. State law prohibits testimony presented at the hearing from being used in a later civil lawsuit, except by court order and except that the Minnesota Department of Human Rights may use evidence presented at the hearing to bring a claim of discrimination against the employer.[478] However, other information provided by the employer or claimant, while private data under the Minnesota Data Practices Act,[479] may be disseminated by the Department to certain other state and federal agencies for use in the administration of their laws and programs (such as tax, labor, welfare, health, etc.)[480]

Even though the evidence at the hearing is protected, most of the information presented at the hearing would be available to the employee/former employee through his or her personnel file or through formal discovery during the pre-litigation phase of a lawsuit. Nevertheless, given the liberal procedures for obtaining evidence during a contested unemployment insurance claim hearing, the employee/former employee will be able to gain information from the employer more easily than in a subsequent lawsuit, Therefore, an employer who does not contest a claim for benefits where grounds exist may have to pay unemployment insurance benefits. However, that employer also avoids the risk of providing information or inconsistencies, or revealing defenses that would be more damaging to the employer in later litigation.

In summary, contesting a claim for unemployment insurance benefits can be costly. Employers are well advised to maintain good personnel records and document any action adverse to the employee and events of misconduct or other work violations. In preparing a response to a claim for benefits, the employee/former employee's personnel file should be reviewed and potential witnesses interviewed so that a complete, accurate and consistent statement results. Putting the facts into one or more of the categories described above may be difficult and, in such situations, legal counsel should be consulted.

ENDNOTES

1   For more information about employee or independent contractor status, consult Internal Revenue Service Publication 15-A "Employer's Supplemental Tax Guide" (Rev. January 2008).

2   Neve v. Austin Daily Herald, 552 N.W.2d 45 (Minn. Ct. App. 1996).

3   26 USC § 3121(d)(3)(A) - (D) (2007).

4   26 USC § 3508 (2007).

5   Minn. Stat. § 181.723 (2008).

6   Minn. Stat. § 363A.08 subd. 4(3) (2007).

7   41 C.F.R. § 60-1.3 (2007) (The "Internet Applicant Rule").

8   U.S. Department of Justice, The Americans with Disabilities Act: Title I Technical Assistance Manual § 3.1, 3.6 (1992).

9   It is recommended that employers do not inquire into employment history further back than the previous five years to avoid an indirect inquiry into age, although it is not legally prohibited. The Age Discrimination in Employment Act (ADEA) only prohibits employment discrimination based on old age (at least 40) and, therefore, does not prohibit employers from favoring relatively older individuals. See Federal Register, July 6, 2007 Volume 72, Number 129; General Dynamics Land Systems, Inc. v. Chine, 540 U.S. 581 (2004). But the Minnesota Human Rights Act (MHRA) protects individuals over the age of majority. Minn. Stat. § 363A.03. Covered employers must comply with both state and federal law.

10 38 USC § 4311 (2007)

11 It is permissible, however, to ask the applicant whether he or she is a U.S. veteran, and the employer may use veteran status as a factor in hiring and may also give special consideration to Vietnam era veterans.

12 This question is acceptable after the applicant becomes an employee.

13 Questions about criminal convictions are permissible if reasonably related to the job for which the applicant is applying. Further, for certain jobs, background checks are required. See discussion under the heading "Background Checks."

14 U.S. Department of Justice, The American with Disabilities Act: Title I Technical Assistance Manual § 5.5(b) (1992).

15 Minn. Stat. § 181.64, 181.65 (2007).

16 Minn. Stat. § 181.635 subd. 2-4 (2007).

17 41 C.F.R. § 60-1.12 (2007). The OFCCP amended its record-keeping requirements in 2006.

18 Minn. Rules § 5000.3420 subp. 1 (2007); Minn. Rules § 5000.3410 subp. 2 (2007); Minn. Stat. § 363A.36 subd. 1(a) (2007).

19 St. Paul Ordinance § 183.04.

20 Minneapolis Code of Ordinances Title 7, Chapter 139.50.

21 Minn. Stat. §§ 326.336 subd. 1; 148A.03(a)(2) (2007).

22 Minn. Stat. § 123B.03 (2007).

23 Minn. Stat. §§ 299C.67 et seq. (2007).

24 Minn. Stat. § 144A.46, subd. 5(b) (2007).

25 U.S. Department of Justice, The Americans with Disabilities Act: Title I Technical Assistance Manual § 5.5(g) (1992).

26 15 U.S.C. §§ 1681 et. seq. (2007).

27 Minn. Stat. § 13C.001 et. seq. (2007).

28 15 U.S.C. §§ 1681b, 1681k (2007); Minn. Stat. § 13C.02 (2007).

29 Minn. Stat. § 363A.20, subd. 8(a)(3) (2007).

30 42 U.S.C. § 2000e (2007); 29 C.F.R. §§ 1607.1 et. seq. (2007).

31 State by Spannaus v. Century Camera, Inc., 309 N.W.2d 735 (Minn. 1981).

[32] 29 U.S.C. § 2002; Minn. Stat. § 181.75 (2007).

[33] Minn. Stat. § 363A.20, subd. 8(a)(1) (2007).

[34] Minn. Stat § 363A.08, subd. 6 (2007).

[35] Minn. Stat § 363A.20, subd. 8(c) (2007).

[36] Minn. Stat § 181.951, subd. 2 (2007).

[37] Minn. Stat §§ 181.951, subd. 2; 363A.20, subd. 8(c) (2007).

[38] 49 C.F.R. §§ 382.101 et. seq. (2007).

[39] Minn. Stat. §§ 181.960-.966 (2007).

[40] Minn. Stat. § 181.9631 (2007).

[41] 8 U.S.C. § 1324a (2007).

[42] 8 C.F.R. § 274a.2(b)(1)(i)(A) (2007).

[43] 8 C.F.R. § 274a.2(b)(1)(vi)(A) (2007).

[44] 8 C.F.R. § 274a.2(b)(1)(vi)(A)(3) (2007).

[45] 8 C.F.R. § 274a.2(b)(1)(vii) (2007).

[46] 8 U.S.C. § 1324a (b)(3) (2007).

[47] Id.

[48] 8 C.F.R. § 274a.10(b)(1)(ii)(A-C) (2007).

[49] 8 U.S.C. § 1324a(f) (2007).

[50] Minn. Exec. Order No. 08-01 (Jan. 7, 2008).

[51] Minn. Exec. Order No. 08-01, 3 (Jan. 7, 2008).

[52] 8 C.F.R. § 214.6 (2007).

[53] Minn. Stat. § 256.998, subd. 3, 5 (2007)

[54] Minn. Stat. § 518A.53, subd. 3 (2007).

[55] Minn. Stat. § 518A.53, subd. 5(a) (2007).

[56] Minn. Stat. § 518A.53, subd. 9(a) (2007) (citing 15 U.S.C. § 1673 (b)(2)).

[57] Minn. Stat. § 518A.53, subd. 5(f) (2007).

[58] Minn. Stat. § 518A.41, subd. 6 (2007).

[59] Webb Publ'g Co. v. Fosshage, 426 N.W.2d 445 (Minn. Ct. App. 1988).

[60] Bennett v. Storz Broadcasting Co., 270 Minn. 525, 534; 134 N.W.2d 892, 899 (1965).

[61] Burke v. Fine, 608 N.W.2d 909 (Minn. Ct. App. 2000), rev denied June 13, 2000.

[62] Davies & Davies Agency, Inc. v. Davies, 298 N.W.2d 127, n.1 (Minn. 1980).

[63] Kallok v. Medtronic, Inc., 573 N.W.2d 356 (Minn. 1998).

[64] 17 U.S.C. § 102(a) (2007).

[65] H.R. Rep. No. 1476, 94th Cong.2d Sess.51 (1976).

[66] Feist Publ'ns, Inc. v. Rural Tel. Serv. Co., 499 U.S. 340, 344(1991).

[67] 17 U.S.C. § 102(a) (2007).

[68] 17 U.S.C. § 101 (2007).

[69] 17 U.S.C. § 204(a) (2007).

[70] PFS Distrib. Co. v. Raduechel, 332 F. Supp.2d 1236, 1248 (S.D. Iowa 2004).

[71] Kirk v. Harker, 188 F.3d 1005, 1007-08 (8th Cir. 1999).

[72] 17 U.S.C. § 101 (2007).

[73] Id.

[74] 17 U.S.C. § 101 (2007).

[75] 17 U.S.C. § 204(a) (2007).

[76] Banks v. Unisys Corp., 228 F.3d 1357, 1359 (Fed. Cir. 2000).

[77] Univ. Patents, Inc. v. Kligman, 762 F. Supp. 1212, 1220 (E.D. Pa. 1991).

78 Miller v. Miller, 222 N.W.2d 71 (Minn. 1965).

79 Minn. Stat. § 181.78 (2007).

80 Id.

81 35 U.S.C. § 101 *et seq.* (2007).

82 35 U.S.C. § 102(b) (2007).

83 Minnesota Mining and Mfg. Co. v. Appleton Papers, Inc., 35 F. Supp.2d 1138 (D. Minn. 1999).

84 Minn. Stat. § 325C.01, subd. 5 (2007).

85 18 U.S.C. § 1830 et seq.

86 *Compare* Cenveo Corp. v. CelumSolutions Software GMBH & Co., 504 F.Supp.2d 574 (D. Minn. 2007) (no injunction or damages available unless computer access caused interruption of computer service) *to* Southwest Airlines Co. v. Farechase, Inc., 318 F. Supp. 2d 435, 439 (N.D. Texas 2004) (allegation of $5,000 loss sufficient to state claim).

87 Minn. Stat. § 338.18 et seq. (2007).

88 Connelly v. Valuevision Media, Inc., 73 U.S. P. Q.2d 1843 (D. Minn. 2005).

89 29 U.S.C. § 206 (2008) (Federal Fair Labor Standards Act).

90 Minn. Stat. § 177.24 (2007).

91 Id.

92 29 U.S.C. § 206 (a) (2007); Minn. Stat. § 177.24, subd. 1(b)(2007).

93 Minn. Stat. § 177.24, subd. 1(c) (2007); 29 USC § 206(g) (2007).

94 Minn. Stat. § 177.24, subd. 2 (2007).

95 Minn. Stat. § 177.24, subd. 3 (2007).

96 Minn. Stat. § 181.06, subd. 2 (2007).

97 Minn. Stat. § 177.24, subd. 4 (2007).

98 Minn. Stat. § 181.79 (2007).

99 29 C.F.R. § 785.14-.17 (2007); Minn. Rules § 5200.0120, subp. 1 & 2 (2007).

100 29 C.F.R. § 785.16(a) (2007); Minn. Rules § 5200.0120, subp. 3 (2007).

101 29 C.F.R. § 785.17 (2007); Minn. Rules § 5200.0120, subp. 2 (2007).

102 29 C.F.R. § 785.22 (2007); Minn. Rules § 5200.0121, subp. 2 (2007).

103 Minn. Stat. § 177.254 (2007).

104 29 C.F.R. § 785.19 (a) (2007); Minn. Rules § 5200.0120, subp. 4 (2007).

105 Minn. Rules § 5200.0060 (2007).

106 Minn. Stat. § 177.253, subd. 1 (2007).

107 Minn. Stat. § 181.939 (2007).

108 29 C.F.R. §§ 785.39, 785.41 (2007).

109 29 U.S.C. § 207 (2007).

110 Minn. Stat. § 177.25, subd. 1 (2007).

111 Minn. Stat. § 177.25, subd. 2, 3, 4 (2007).

112 29 C.F.R. Part 541 et seq. (2007). Individuals employed in bona fide executive, administrative, professional or outside sales positions are not considered "employees" under Minnesota's FLSA. Minn. Stat. § 177.23, subd. 7 (6) (2007).

113 29 C.F.R. § 541.600(d) (2007).

114 29 C.F.R. § 541.2 (2007).

115 29 C.F.R. §§ 541.100-300 (2007); Minn. Rules § 5200.0180, subd. 1 (2007).

116 29 C.F.R. § 541.3 (2007).

117 29 C.F.R. § 541.601 (2007).

118 29 C.F.R. § 541.600 (a) (2007).

119 29 C.F.R. § 541.602 (2007).

120 29 C.F.R. § 541.602 (b) (7) (2007); 29 C.F.R. § 825.206 (2007).

121 Minn. Stat. § 181A.07 (2007).

[122] Minn. Stat. § 181A.04, subd. 6 (2007).

[123] Minn. Stat § 181A.04 (2007); 29 C.F.R. § 570.122 (2007).

[124] Minn. Stat. § 181A.06, subd. 1 (2007).

[125] 29 C.F.R. § 570.121 (2007).

[126] Minn. Rules § 5200.0010 (2007).

[127] Minn. Stat. § 181.10 (2007).

[128] Minn. Stat. § 181.101 (2007).

[129] Minn. Stat. § 181.101 (2007).

[130] Minn. Stat. § 471.426 (2007).

[131] Minn. Stat. § 177.27, subd. 2 (2007).

[132] Minn. Stat. § 177.27, subd. 7 (2007).

[133] Minn. Stat. § 177.30 (2007); 29 C.F.R. § 516.2 (2007).

[134] Minn. Stat. § 181.032 (2007).

[135] ERISA § 3(2); 29 USC § 1002(2)

[136] ERISA § 3(1); 29 USC § 1002(1)

[137] I.R.C. §§ 401 et. seq.; 26 USC §§ 401 et. seq.

[138] See I.R.C. §§ 104-106, 125; 26 USC §§ 104-106, 125

[139] For example, I.R.C. §§ 4975, 4980B; 26 U.S.C. §§ 4975, 4980B

[140] ERISA, Title I, Parts 1-3; 29 USC §§ 1021-1085

[141] ERISA, Title I, Part 4; 29 USC §§ 1101-1114

[142] ERISA, Title I, Part 5; 29 USC §§ 1131-1148

[143] ERISA § 404(a)(1)(A)-(D); 29 USC § 1104(a)(1)(A)-(D)

[144] ERISA § 410(b); 29 USC § 1110(b); M.S.A. 302A.521

[145] ERISA § 412; 29 USC § 1112

[146] ERISA § 606(a)(1); 29 USC § 1166(a)(1)

[147] ERISA § 104(b)(1)(A); 29 USC § 1024(b)(1)(A)

[148] ERISA § 104(b)(1); 29 USC § 1024(b)(1)

[149] ERISA § 105; 29 USC § 1025

[150] ERISA § 104(a)(1); 29 USC § 1024(a)(1)

[151] ERISA § 503; 29 USC § 1133; 29 CFR § 2560.503-1

[152] LaRue v. DeWolff, Boberg & Assocs, Inc. (2008 S.Ct) 2008 WL.440748

[153] Pub. L. No. 99-272 (Apr. 7, 1986)

[154] Minn. Stat. § 62A.17, § 61A.092 (2005).

[155] ERISA § 601(b); PHSA §2201(b)(1); See I.R.C. § 4980B(d)(1); 29 U.S.C. § 1161(b) (2007).

[156] See I.R.C. § 4980B(d).

[157] I.R.C. § 213(d)

[158] Treas. Reg. § 54.4980B-2, Q/A-1(a), Q/A-8.

[159] ERISA § 603; I.R.C. §4980B(f)(3); Treas. Reg. § 54.4980B-4, Q/A-1; 29 U.S.C. § 1163 (2007).

[160] Treas. Reg. § 54.4980B-4, Q/A-1(c).

[161] Treas. Reg. § 54.4980B-10, Q/A-1(a).

[162] Treas. Reg. § 54.4980B-10, Q/A-2, Example 2.

[163] Treas. Reg. § 54.4980B-10, Q/A-4.

[164] ERISA § 601(a); I.R.C. § 4980B(f)(1); PHSA § 2201(a); 29 U.S.C. § 1161(a) (2007).

[165] ERISA § 605(a)(2); I.R.C. § 4980B(f)(5)(B); PHSA § 2205(a)(2); 29 U.S.C. § 1165(a)(2) (2007).

[166] ERISA § 602(2)(A); I.R.C. § 4980B(f)(2)(B)(i); PHSA § 2202(2)(A); 29 U.S.C. § 1165(2)(A) (2007).

[167] I.R.C. § 4980B(f)(2)(B)(i) (2007).

[168] ERISA § 602(2)(B)-(E); I.R.C. § 4980B(f)(2)(B)(ii)-(v); PHSA § 2202(2)(B)-(E); 29 U.S.C. § 1162(2)(B)-(E) (2007).

[169] ERISA § 606(a)(1); I.R.C. § 4980B(f)(6)(A); PHSA § 2206(1); 29 U.S.C. § 1166(a)(1) (2007).

[170] 69 Fed. Reg. 30084 (May 26, 2004).

[171] 29 C.F.R. § 2590.606-1

[172] 29 C.F.R. § 2590.606-1(c).

[173] 29 C.F.R. § 2590.606-4.

[174] 29 C.F.R. § 2590.606-4(b)(4).

[175] 29 C.F.R. § 2590.606-4(d).

[176] 29 C.F.R. § 2590.606-4(c).

[177] ERISA 606(a)(2); I.R.C. § 4980B(f)(6)(B); PHSA § 2206(2); 29 C.F.R. § 2590.606-2(b)(3); 29 U.S.C. § 1166(a)(2) (2007).

[178] 29 C.F.R. § 2590.606-3.

[179] 29 C.F.R. § 2590.606-3(b)(2).

[180] ERISA § 605(a)(1); I.R.C. § 4980B(f)(5); PHSA §2205(a)(1); 29 U.S.C. § 1165(a)(1) (2007).

[181] Kerr v. Chicago Transit Authority, 1998 U.S. Dist. LEXIS 2166 (N.D. Ill. 1998).

[182] ERISA § 605(a)(2); I.R.C. §4980B(f)(5)(B); PHSA §2205(a)(2); 29 U.S.C. § 1165(a)(2) (2007).

[183] Treas. Reg. § 54.4980B-6, Q/A-6.

[184] Treas. Reg. § 54.4980B-8, Q/A-1(a).

[185] ERISA § 602(3)(A); 29 U.S.C. § 1162(3)(A) (2007).

[186] ERISA § 602(3); 29 U.S.C. § 1162(3) (2007).

[187] ERISA § 602(3); Treas. Reg. §54.4980B-8, Q/A-5(b); 29 U.S.C. § 1162(3) (2007).

[188] ERISA § 602(2)(C); Treas. Reg. §54.4980B-8, Q/A-5(a); 29 U.S.C. § 1162(2)(C) (2007).

[189] IRC § 4980B(b)(1).

[190] IRC § 4980B(c)(4).

[191] ERISA §§ 502(a)(1)(A), 502(c)(1)(A); 29 C.F.R. § 2575.502c-3; 29 U.S.C. § 1132(a)(1)(A), 1132(c)(1)(A) (2007).

[192] ERISA § 502(c); 29 U.S.C. § 1132(c) (2007).

[193] ERISA § 502(g); 29 U.S.C. § 1132(g) (2007).

[194] Minn. Stat. §§ 62A.16, 62A.17 (2005).

[195] Minn. Stat. § 62A.17, subd. 1 (2005).

[196] Minn. Stat. § 62A.17, subd. 2 (2005).

[197] Minn. Stat. § 62A.17, subd. 5 (2005).

[198] Minn. Stat. § 62A.17, subd. 6 (2005).

[199] Minn. Stat. § 61A.092, subd. 1 (2005).

[200] Minn. Stat. § 61A.092, subd. 2 (2005).

[201] Minn. Stat. § 61A.092, subd. 3 (2005).

[202] Minn. Stat. § 61A.092, subd. 5 (2005).

[203] Pub. L. No. 104-191 (Aug. 21, 1996).

[204] I.R.C. § 9801(a); ERISA § 701(a); PHSA § 2701(a); 29 U.S.C. § 1181(a) (2007).

[205] I.R.C. § 9801(b)(3)(A); ERISA § 701(b)(3)(A); PHSA § 2701(b)(3)(A); 29 U.S.C. § 1181(b)(3)(A) (2007).

[206] ERISA § 701(e)(1)(A); PHSA § 2701(e)(1)(A); I.R.C. § 9801(e)(1); 29 U.S.C. § 1181(e)(1)(A) (2007).

[207] 69 Fed. Reg. 78720-01.

[208] 45 C.F.R. § 160.103; 45 C.F.R. §164.104 (2005).

[209] 45 C.F.R. § 160.103 (2005).

[210] 45 C.F.R. § 160.103 (2005).

[211] 45 C.F.R. § 164.502 (2005).

[212] 45 C.F.R. § 164.508 (2005).

[213] 45 C.F.R. § 164.512 (2005).

[214] 45 C.F.R. §§ 164.520-28 (2005).

[215] 45 C.F.R. § 164.520 (2005).

[216] 45 C.F.R. § 164.530 (2005).

[217] 45 C.F.R. § 164.502(e) (2005).

[218] 45 C.F.R. § 160.103 (2005).

[219] 45 C.F.R. § 164.530(k) (2005).

[220] SSA §1176.

[221] SSA § 1177.

[222] Minn. Stat. § 363A.08, subd. 2 (2007).

[223] 42 U.S.C. § 2000e et seq. (2007); 29 U.S.C. § 621 et seq. (2007).

[224] 42 U.S.C. § 12101 et seq. (2007).

[225] Walters v. Metro. Educ. Enter., Inc., 519 U.S. 202 (1997); EEOC Notice, Number 915.002, December 3, 1997; 42 U.S.C. § 2000e(b) (2007).

[226] Reeves v. Sanderson Plumbing Prods, Inc., 530 U.S. 133 (2000); St. Mary's Honor Center v. Hicks, 509 U.S. 502 (1993); Hoover v. Norwest Private Mortgage Banking, 632 N.W. 2d 534, 546 (Minn. 2001).

[227] Minn. Stat. § 363A.20 (2007).

[228] Minn. Stat. § 363A.03, subd. 12 (2007).

[229] Minn. Stat. § 363A.03, subd. 36 (2007).

[230] Minn. Stat. § 363A.08, subd. 6 (2007).

[231] 42 U.S.C. § 12101 et seq. (2007).

[232] U.S. Department of Justice, The Americans with Disabilities Act: Title I Technical Assistance Manual § 1.1 (1992).

[233] Chevron U.S.A. v. Echazabal, 536 U.S. 73 (2002).

[234] U.S. Airways v. Barnett 535 U.S. 391 (2002).

[235] 42 U.S.C. § 12102 (2008).

[236] Toyota Motor Mfg, Ky. Inc. v. Williams, 534 U.S. 184 (2002).

[237] See Sutton v. United Air Lines, Inc., 527 U.S. 471 (1999).

[238] 29 C.F.R. § 1630.1 et seq. (2007); Id. App. (2005).

[239] Bragdon v. Sidney Abbott, 524 U.S. 624 (1998).

[240] Minn. Stat. § 363A.03, subd. 36 (2007).

[241] Minn. Stat. § 62A.149 (2007).

[242] Minn. Stat. § 181.950 et seq. (2007).

[243] Minn. Stat. § 363A.20, subd. 8 (2007).

[244] 41 U.S.C. § 701, et seq. (2007).

[245] Minn. Stat. § 181.938, subd. 2 (2007).

[246] Minn. Stat. § 181.81, subd. 1 (2007).

[247] 29 U.S.C. § 630(b) (2007).

[248] O'Connor v. Consolidated Coin Caterers Corp., 517 U.S. 308 (1996).

[249] Minn. Stat. § 363A.31 (2007).

[250] Older Workers Benefit Protection Act § 201, 29 U.S.C. § 626(f)(1) (2007).

[251] Oubre v. Entergy Operations, Inc., 522 U.S. 422 (1998).

[252] Novack v. Northwest Airlines, Inc., 525 N.W.2d 592, 598 (Minn. Ct. App. 1995).

[253] Int'l Union, United Auto., Aerospace and Agric. Implement Workers of Am., UAW v. Johnson Controls, Inc., 499 U.S. 187 (1991).

[254] 29 U.S.C. § 206 (2007).

[255] Minn. Stat. § 181.66 et seq. (2007).

[256] Minn. Stat. § 181.67, subd. 1 (2007).

[257] See Costilla v. Minnesota, 571 N.W.2d 587 (Minn. Ct. App. 1997).

258 See Oncale v. Sundowner Offshore Servs. Inc., 523 U.S. 75 (1998); Cummings v. Koehnen, 568 N.W.2d 418 (Minn. 1997).

259 See Faragher v. City of Boca Raton, 524 U.S. 775 (1998); Burlington Indus. Inc. v. Ellerth, 524 U.S. 742 (1998).

260 Guiliani v. Stuart Corp., 512 N.W.2d 589, 595 (Minn. Ct. App. 1994).

261 Minn. Stat § 363A.08, subd. 1 (2007).

262 Minneapolis, Minn. Ordinance Ch. 139.40 (2007); St. Paul, Minn. Leg. Code Ch. 183.01, 183.02(26) (2007).

263 Goins v. West Group, 635 N.W.2d 717 (Minn. 2001).

264 Minn. Stat. § 363A.03, subd. 44 (2007).

265 Minn. Stat. § 363A.26 (2007).

266 Minn. Stat. § 363A.20, subd. 3 (2007).

267 Minn. Stat. § 363A.08, subd. 2 (2007).

268 Minn. Stat. § 363A.03, subd. 24 (2007).

269 Counters v. Farmland Indus., Inc., No. C3-88-1158, 1988 WL 134800 (Minn. Ct. App. Dec. 20, 1988).

270 Minn. Stat. § 181.932, subd. 1 (2007).

271 Anderson-Johanningmeier v. Mid-Minnesota Women's Ctr. Inc., 637 N.W.2d 270 (Minn. 2002).

272 Burlington Northern & Santa Fe RR Co. v. White, 548 U.S. 53 (2006).

273 Id.

274 Id.

275 See Robinson v. Shell Oil Co., 519 U.S. 337 (1997).

276 Minn. Stat. § 181.938, subd. 2 (2007).

277 Minn. Stat. § 144.414 (2007).

278 Minn. Stat. § 144.413 (2007).

279 Minn. Stat. § 144.413 (2007).

280 Minn. Stat. § 144.4167, subd. 3–7 (2007).

281 Minn. Stat. § 144.416 (2007).

282 Minn. Stat. § 144.416 (2007).

283 Minn. Stat. § 144.417, subd. 2(a) (2007).

284 Minn. Stat. § 144.417, subd. 2(d) (2007).

285 Minn. Stat. § 144.417, subd. 4 (2007).

286 Minn. Stat. § 181.938, subd. 2 (2007).

287 29 U.S.C. § 2002 et seq. (2007); Minn. Stat. § 181.75, subd. 1 (2007).

288 State by Spannaus v. Century Camera, Inc., 309 N.W.2d 735 (Minn. 1981).

289 Minn. Stat. § 181.76 (2007).

290 Minn. Stat. § 571.72 (2007).

291 Minn. Stat. § 571.922 (2007).

292 Minn. Stat. § 571.927 (2007).

293 Circuit City Stores v. Adams, 532 U.S. 105 (2001).

294 EEOC v. Waffle House, Inc., 534 U.S. 279 (2002).

295 Correll v. Distinctive Dental Servs., P.A., 607 N.W.2d 440 (Minn. 2000).

296 Feges v. Perkins Restaurants, Inc., 483 N.W.2d 701 (Minn. 1992); Pine River State Bank v. Mettille, 333 N.W.2d 622 (Minn. 1983).

297 Minn. Stat. § 181.937 (2007).

298 29 U.S.C. § 158 (a)(3) (2007); Minn. Stat. § 179.12 (2007).

299 Price Waterhouse v. Hopkins, 490 U.S. 228 (1989).

300 29 U.S.C. § 2601 et seq. (2007); 29 C.F.R. § 825.100 et. seq. (2007).

301 29 C.F.R. § 825.105 (2007).

302 Ragsdale v. Wolverine World Wide, Inc., 535 U.S. 81 (2002).

303 29 U.S.C. § 2612 (2008).

304 29 U.S.C. § 2612(a)(1)(E) (2008).

305 http://www.federalregister.gov/OFRUpload/OFRData/2008-26577_PI.pdf, p. 95.

306 http://www.federalregister.gov/OFRUpload/OFRData/2008-26577_PI.pdf, p. 95.

307 29 U.S.C. § 2612(e)(3) (2008).

308 29 U.S.C. § 2612(a)(3) (2008).

309 29 U.S.C. § 2611(16) (2008).

310 29 U.S.C. § 2613(f) (2008).

311 Minn. Stat. § 181.948 (2007).

312 Minn. Stat. § 181.947 (2007).

313 Minn. Stat. § 181.940, subd. 2; § 181.941, subd. 1 (2007).

314 Minn. Stat. § 181.9413 (2007).

315 Minn. Stat. § 181.945 (2007).

316 Minn. Stat. § 181.9412 (2007).

317 Lee v. Fresenius Medical Care, Inc., 741 N.W.2d 117 (Minn. 2007).

318 Lee v. Fresenius Medical Care, Inc., 741 N.W.2d 117 (Minn. 2007).

319 Minn. Stat. § 181.74, subd. 1 (2007).

320 38 U.S.C. § 4301 et seq. (2007); see also Minn. Stat. § 181.946 (2007) (Employers must also allow unpaid leave for civil air patrol service as long as the leave would not unduly disrupt the operations of the employer.).

321 Minn. Stat. § 593.50 (2007).

322 Minn. Stat. § 204C.04 (2007).

323 Minn. Stat. § 204B.195 (2007).

324 Minn. Stat. § 177.254 (2007).

325 Minn. Stat. § 177.253 (2007).

326 Minn. Stat. § 181.939 (2007).

327 Minn. Stat. §§ 181.960-.966 (2007).

328 Minn. Stat. § 181.9631 (2007).

329 Minn. Stat. § 181.980, subd. 2 (2007).

330 Minn. Stat. § 181.980, subd. 3 (2007).

331 Minn. Stat. § 181.980, subd. 5 (2007).

332 Lake v. Wal-Mart Stores, Inc., 582 N.W.2d 231 (Minn. 1998).

333 18 U.S.C. § 2510 et seq. (2007); Minn. Stat. § 626A.01 et. seq. (2007).

334 Minn. Stat. §§ 302A.251, subd. 1, 302A.361 (2007).

335 Gunderson v. Alliance of Computer Prof'l, Inc., 628 N.W. 2d 173 (Minn. Ct. App. 2001).

336 Minn. Stat. § 302A.461 (2007).

337 Minn. Stat. § 302A.751, subd. 3a (2007).

338 Minn. Stat. §§ 322B.663, 322B. 69, 322B.833, subd. 4 (2007).

339 Minn. Stat. § 176.021 (2007).

340 Minn. Stat. § 176.011, subd. 10 (2007).

341 Minn. Stat. §176.041 (2007).

342 Minn. Stat. § 176.181, subd. 2 (2007).

343 Minn. Stat. § 176.181, subd. 2 (2007).

344 Minn. Stat. § 176.181, subd. 3 (2007).

345 Minn. Stat. § 176.031 (2007).

346 Minn. Stat. § 79.081 (2007).

347 Minn. Stat. § 79.53 et seq. (2007) (setting forth procedures for premium calculation).

[348] Minn. Stat. § 176.139 (2007).

[349] Minn. Stat. § 176.231 (2007).

[350] 29 C.F.R. § 1904.39(a) (2007).

[351] Minn. Stat. § 176.101, .111, .135 (2007).

[352] Minn. Rules Chapter 5223 (2007).

[353] Minn. Stat. § 176.82, subd. 2 (2007).

[354] Minn. Stat. § 176.239 (2007).

[355] Minn. Stat. § 176.2615 (2007).

[356] Minn. Stat. § 176.82 (2007).

[357] Minn. Stat. § 176.1351 (2007).

[358] Minn. Stat. § 182.65, subd. 2 (2007).

[359] See, e.g., Minn. R. Chap. 5206 (2007).

[360] Minn. Stat. § 182.652, subd. 1-2 (2007).

[361] Minn. Stat. § 182.653 (2007).

[362] Minn. Stat. § 182.655, subd. 2 (2007).

[363] Minn. Stat. § 182.655, subd. 5 (2007).

[364] Minn. Stat. § 182.668 (2007).

[365] Minn. Stat. § 182.658 (2007).

[366] Minn. Stat. § 182.655, subd. 10a (2007).

[367] Minn. Stat. § 182.663 (2007).

[368] Minn. Stat. § 182.666 (2007).

[369] Minn. Stat. §§ 182.654, subd. 8; 182.659, subd. 4 (2007).

[370] Minn. Stat. § 182.654, subd. 3 (2007).

[371] Minn. Stat. § 182.654, subd. 4-6 (2007).

[372] Minn. Stat. § 182.659, subd. 3 (2007).

[373] Minn. Stat. § 182.654, subd. 9 (2007).

[374] Minn. R. 5210.0470, subd. 2; Minn. Stat. § 182.659, subd. 1 (2007).

[375] Minn. Stat. § 182.659, subd. 1 (2007).

[376] Minn. Stat. § 182.659, subd. 3 (2007).

[377] Minn. Stat. § 182.659, subd. 3 (2007); Minn. R. 5210.0490 (2007).

[378] Id.

[379] Minn. R. 5210.0490 (2007).

[380] Minn. Stat. § 182.659, subd. 3 (2007); Minn. R. 5210.0500 (2007).

[381] See, Minn. Stat. § 182.659, subd. 6 (2007).

[382] See, Minn. Stat. § 182.659, subd. 1 (2007); Minn. R. 5210.0470 (2007).

[383] Minn. Stat. § 182.659, subd. 1 (2007)

[384] Minn. R. 5210.0470 (2007).

[385] See, Minn. Stat. § 182.668 (2007); Minn. R. 5210.0510 (2007).

[386] See, Minn. Stat. § 182.668 (2007).

[387] Minn. R. 5210.0480 (2007).

[388] Minn. R. 5210.0470, subd. 5 (2007).

[389] Minn. Stat. § 182.66, subd. 1 (2007).

[390] Minn. Stat. § 182.661, subd. 1 (2007).

[391] Minn. Stat. § 182.66, subd. 1 (2007)

[392] See, Minn. R. 5210.0470, subd. 5 (2007).

[393] Minn. Stat. § 182.661, subd. 1 (2007).

[394] Minn. Stat. § 182.661, subd. 3 (2007).

[395] Minn. Stat. § 182.654, subd. 9 (2007).

[396] Id.

[397] Minn. Stat. § 182.654, subd. 11 (2007).

[398] Id.

[399] Minn. Stat. § 182.669 (2007).

[400] Id.

[401] See, Minn. Stat. § 182.653, 4a-4f (2007).

[402] Minn. R. 5206.0200 (2007).

[403] Minn. Stat. § 182.653, subd. 4(j) (2007).

[404] Minn. R. 5206.1000 (2007).

[405] Minn. R. 5206.0300 (2007).

[406] Id.

[407] Minn. Stat. § 182.653, subd. 4a-4f (2007).

[408] Id.

[409] Minn. R. 5206.0400-.0600 (2007).

[410] Minn. Stat. §§ 144.411 to 144.417 (2005).

[411] Minn. Stat. § 144.414 (2005).

[412] Minn. Stat. § 144.414 (2007).

[413] Minn. Stat. § 182.653, subd 9 (2007); Minn. R. 5208.1500 (2007)

[414] Minn. Stat. § 182.653, subd. 9 (2007).

[415] Minn. Stat. § 182.653, subd. 8 (2007).

[416] Id.

[417] 29 U.S.C. § 2101 et seq. (2007).

[418] Minn. Stat. § 116L.976 (2007).

[419] In the opinion of the Minnesota Supreme Court, " '[a] work force reduction situation occurs when business considerations cause an employer to eliminate one or more positions within the company. An employee is not eliminated as a part of a workforce reduction when he or she is replaced after his or her discharge. However, a person is not replaced when another employee is assigned to perform the plaintiff's duties in addition to other duties, or when the work is redistributed among other existing employees already performing related work. A person is replaced only when another person is hired or reassigned to perform the plaintiff's duties.' " Dietrich v. Canadian Pacific Ltd., 536 N.W.2d 319, 324 (Minn. 1995).

[420] 29 U.S.C. § 2101 et seq. (2007).

[421] Minn. Stat. § 116L.976 (2007).

[422] Minn. Stat. § 181.81 (2007).

[423] Minn. Stat. § 363A et seq. (2007).

[424] 42 U.S.C. § 12101 et seq. (2007).

[425] 29 U.S.C. § 215(a)(3) (2007); Minn. Stat. § 177.21 et seq. (2007).

[426] 29 U.S.C. § 158(a); Minn. Stat. § 179.12 (2007).

[427] 29 U.S.C. § 660(c) (2007); Minn. Stat. § 182.669 et seq. (2007).

[428] Minn. Stat. § 176.82, subd. 1 (2007).

[429] 29 U.S.C. § 1140 et seq. (2007).

[430] 29 U.S.C. § 2615 (2007); Minn. Stat. § 181.941 (2007).

[431] Minn. Stat. § 181.937 (2007).

[432] Minn. Stat. § 571.927, subd. 1 (2007).

[433] Minn. Stat. § 626.556, subd. 4a (2007).

[434] Minn. Stat. § 181.52 (2007).

[435] Minn. Stat. § 181.932, subd. 1 (2007).

[436] Minn. Stat. § 593.50, subd. 1 (2007).

[437] Minn. Stat. § 181.964 (2007).

[438] Reeves v. Sanderson Plumbing Products, Inc., 530 U.S. 133 (2000).

[439] Minn. Stat. § 181.933 (2007).

[440] Minn. Stat. § 363A.31 (2007).

[441] 29 U.S.C. § 626(F), (G) (2007).

[442] Minn. Stat. § 609.27, subd. 1(5) (2007).

[443] Minn. Stat. § 181.13(a) (2007).

[444] Minn. Stat. § 181.13(b) (2007).

[445] Minn. Stat. § 181.14, subd. 1 (2007).

[446] Minn. Stat. § 181.145, subd. 2(b) (2007).

[447] Minn. Stat. § 181.933, subd. 1 (2007).

[448] Minn. Stat. § 181.967 (2007).

[449] Minn. Stat. §§ 181.967, subd. 4, 13.43 (2007).

[450] Minn. Stat. § 325E.37 (2007).

[451] Minn. Stat. § 325E.37, subd. 6 (2007).

[452] Minn. Stat. § 268.03 (2007).

[453] Minn. Stat. §§ 268.001 (2007).

[454] Minn. Stat. § 268.035, subd. 14 (2007).

[455] Minn. Stat. § 268.035, subd. 11 (2007).

[456] Minn. Stat. § 268.035, subd. 20 (2007).

[457] Minn. Stat. § 268.035, subd. 9 (2007).

[458] Minn. Stat. §§ 268.035, subd. 14, 268.042 (2007).

[459] Minn. Stat. § 268.065, subd. 2 (2007).

[460] Minn. Stat. § 268.051, subd. 4 (2007).

[461] Minn. Stat. § 268.063(a) (2007).

[462] Minn. Stat. § 268.063(b) (2007).

[463] Minn. Stat. § 268.035, subd. 12, 14, 15 (2007).

[464] Minn. Stat. § 268.035, subd. 15(1) (2007).

[465] Minn. Stat. § 268.035, subd. 20 (2007).

[466] Minn. Stat. § 268.051 (2007).

[467] Id.

[468] Minn. Stat. § 268.047, subd. 2(1) (2007).

[469] Minn. Stat. § 268.051, subd. 3, 7 (2007).

[470] Minn. Stat. § 268.07, subd. 2 (2007).

[471] Minn. Stat. § 268.085, subd. 1, 16(b) (2007).

[472] Minn. Stat. § 268.085, subd. 5(b) (2007).

[473] Minn. Stat. § 268.095, subd. 6 (2007).

[474] Minn. Stat. §§ 268.07, subd. 3a, 268.101, subd. 2(f) (2007).

[475] Minn. Stat. § 268.105, subd. 1 (2007).

[476] Minn. Rules 3310.2901-3310.2925 (2007).

[477] Minn. Stat. § 268.105, subd. 2(a) (2007).

[478] Minn. Stat. § 268.105, subd. 5(c) (2007).

[479] Minn. Stat. §§ 13.02, subd. 9, 268.19, subd. 1 (2007).

[480] Minn. Stat. § 268.19 (2007).